FOOTBALL RULES:
SIMPLY STATED

FOOTBALL RULES: SIMPLY STATED

2014 Edition

11th Edition

A. D. McPhilomy

Copyright © 2013 by A. D. McPhilomy.

ISBN: Softcover   978-1-4836-1675-9
       eBook   978-1-4836-1676-6

All rights reserved. No part of this book may be reproduced or transmitted in any form or by any means, electronic or mechanical, including photocopying, recording, or by any information storage and retrieval system, without permission in writing from the copyright owner.

This book was printed in the United States of America.

Rev. date: 05/13/2014

To order additional copies of this book, contact:
Xlibris LLC
1-888-795-4274
www.Xlibris.com
Orders@Xlibris.com
601624

CONTENTS

Common High School Football Myths 11
New & Important Changes For 2014 15
Dynamic Football Statements 16
The Game, Field, Players & Equipment 20
Player equipment 25
Definitions 30
    Blocking 30
    Conferences 32
    Encroachment 33
    Fair catch 33
    Force 35
    Formations 36
    Forward progress 37
    Fouls & Penalties 37
    Free blocking zone 38
    Kicks 41
    Neutral zone 43
    Player designations 44
    Spots 47
Length of periods 50
Overtime procedure 50
Mercy rule 51
Starting the half/period 51
Ending period/half 52
Starting and stopping the clock 53
Timeouts 54
Officials time-outs 55
Delay of game 56
Substitutions 57
Starting a play 58

Ball becomes dead & down ends	58
Inadvertent whistle	59
Out of bounds spot	60
Series of downs & new series of downs	62
Change of possession plays & series	63
Post scrimmage kick	64
Down & possession after penalty	65
Line to gain and measurements	67
Kickoffs & free kicks	69
Scrimmage kicks	71
Kicks causing a touchback	72
Fair catch	72
Kick Catching Interference	73
Before the snap	74
Encroachment	75
False start	75
Position, numbering & action at the snap	75
Handing the ball	77
Fumble & backward pass	77
Forward pass	78
Pass interference	80
Scoring	82
Touchdown	82
PAT	83
Field goal	84
Force, safety & touchback	85
Player conduct	87
Illegal use of hands/holding	87
Illegal blocks	87
Personal fouls	90
Unsportsmanlike conduct	90
Illegal participation	91
Illegal batting/kicking	91
Non-player unsportsmanlike fouls	92
Penalty Enforcement	95
Loss of down fouls	96
Automatic 1st down fouls	96
Double & multiple fouls	96
Change of possession with fouls	96

Types of plays for penalty enforcement 98
Basic spots of enforcement 98
Special enforcements 100
Penalty chart and enforcement chart 101
"All but one" penalty enforcement 103

INTRODUCTION & ACKNOWLEDGMENTS

This document has been written to simplify high school football rules. It is geared toward football officials but is a valuable guide for coaches, fans, and parents who want to understand the actual rules. The document is a complete statement of high school football rules and is separated into sections. Examples are provided in italics to clarify a rule, especially the rules which govern uncommon circumstances.

In this 2014 edition, the author expresses her sincere appreciation to Ken Dunlap & George Brown from The University of Alabama Recreational Sports Center for the introduction to officiating in 1989; Van Royal for answering all those rules questions back in 1994; her crew mates and partners throughout the years; and especially Kenneth G. Vernoski for being a partner, mentor, best friend and guiding force behind this document.

A. D. McPhilomy
Jacksonville, Florida
Football Official 1989-current
2013 National Collegiate Flag Football Championships
    Hall of Fame Inductee

COMMON HIGH SCHOOL FOOTBALL MYTHS

"The QB threw the ball away outside the tackle . . ." This is an NFL & NCAA rule. In high school football, the QB must throw a pass into an area where an eligible receiver has a possibility of catching the ball. A high school QB can't throw the ball away, especially if he's about to be sacked, unless he throws it near an eligible receiver.

"The pass was un-catchable . . ." This is an NFL & NCAA rule. Pass interference may only occur in the area of potential receivers, beyond the neutral zone. Even if a pass is overthrown, players may not interfere with each other.

"The defense got back on-side before the snap . . ." The NFL & NCAA allow this, but in HS, the defense can't "get back" on-side once they encroach.

"We purposely went on "two" and jerked to a set position on 4th down to get the defense to jump off-side . . ." This is a false start by the offense. The rule states any act clearly intended to make the defense encroach is a false start. On 4th down, the offense can't do any significant new act to make the defense encroach. If a false start causes Team B/R to encroach, only the false start will be penalized.

"When a player on the kicking team touches a punt down field, it is down . . ." This is called 1st touching. If the ball is still rolling, it is alive. It's wiser for the K player to pick up the kick. After K's 1st touching, if

a member of the receiving team picks the 1st touched ball up, he may advance it, and if he loses possession, he still gets the option to take the ball where it was 1st touched. The rationale is that Team K shall not touch a ball they can't legally possess. But forced touching isn't touching.

"Team R touched the kick then it bounced into the end zone. Why was the play ruled a touchback? . . ." Any punt, kickoff, or short/no-good field goal attempt across the receiving team's goal line is a touchback. Even if touched by any player, non-scoring kicks into the receiving team's end zone are always touchbacks.

"The receiver who caught the ball didn't signal fair catch. Why is the ball dead? . . ." If any Team R player signals for a fair catch, the ball becomes dead when any Team R player possesses a kick.

"He took his helmet off . . ." This is not a foul in high school, unless he is trying to direct attention to himself or use it in an unacceptable manner. Yet, if it comes off through play, not caused by an opponent's foul, he must leave the game for one play. No player shall contact a helmet-less player nor shall they attempt to play without their helmet.

"They broke the huddle with 12 players . . ." High school football rules do not state that this is illegal. Once a substitute enters a huddle, the replaced player shall leave within 3 seconds.

"When may linemen go down field on a punt? . . ." Linemen may go down-field immediately after the snap.

"That's a horse-collar tackle . . ." A horse collar tackle must involve the hand(s) on the neck line and the player is pulled down backward, causing him to "fall funny" at risk for knee injury. Just grabbing the collar isn't a foul-it must pull the runner down backward and be the impetus of the tackle.

"The kickoff went 10 yards, so it is a free ball . . ." The ball has to also hit the ground to make this a free ball. Team K can't legally block or possess the ball until it goes 10 yards and touches the ground or an opponent. If Team K "pooch" kicks the ball high and short then catches it before it hits the ground or an opponent, this is kick-catching interference. The receiving team may take the ball at that spot or tack on 15 yards.

"The receiver touched the kick, so a kicking team member may pick it up and advance . . ." For kickoffs, Team K may never advance a kick. If it has gone 10 yards and touched the ground, they may possess and keep it, but may not advance a kick. It will be their ball at the spot of the recovery. On scrimmage kicks (kick plays that started with a snap) Team K may advance the kick if they get it behind the line of scrimmage (like a blocked punt), but they usually must advance for a 1st down. If Team R touches the kick 2+ yards beyond the line of scrimmage, it becomes a free ball and whoever gets it, keeps it, but Team K still can't advance a scrimmage kick beyond the line of scrimmage. But forced touching isn't touching.

"What about the "halo" rule for the player receiving the punt? . . ." This has never been a high school rule, but the receiver has the right to catch the kick without being impeded by the kicking team.

"He "chucked" the receiver more than 5 yards down field? . . ." In high school football, there is no "chuck" distance defined. A defender may legally "chuck" a receiver until the receiver gets beside him. It is legal for the corner to bump the receiver, then the safety to "chuck" him legally (in front) until the ball is released on a forward pass. Until the ball is in flight on a pass, a receiver may be legally "chucked" all the way down field.

"Since we intercepted, why don't we get to keep the ball?" The team in final possession has to get the ball legally to be able to keep it. This is called getting the ball with "clean hands." They have to intercept without any fouls to keep the ball.

"We ran a play with the tackle eligible. What's the flag? . . ." Receivers may catch a pass if wearing #1-49 or 80-99 and is on the end of the line, or is a back. If a tackle has an ineligible number or isn't an end, he can't legally touch a forward pass. Yet, the "A-11" offense developed in California a few years ago is now illegal. In punt or field goal formation, on 1st, 2nd or 3rd downs, there must still be 4 players with ineligible numbers around the center. The center may not be eligible in this formation on these downs. 4th downs, there is no requirement for any ineligible numbers, but interior linemen are still ineligible, even when wearing an eligible number.

"What is an illegal shift? . . ." All 11 offensive players must be set for one second before the snap. If a player wants to go in motion, he and all his team-mates must be set one second, then only he may move. Often a player goes into motion and then linemen get set or the QB goes under center. This is an illegal shift since all 11 players weren't set one second before the man went into motion.

"I didn't see anyone jump. Why was that a false start? . . ." Offensive interior linemen are not allowed to remove both hands from the ground once they've put one down. The snapper can't remove his hand from the ball, nor may he turn the ball end to end or move the ball as in an illegal snap.

NEW & IMPORTANT CHANGES FOR 2014

<u>TARGETING IS DEFINED</u> as taking aim with the helmet, forearm, hand, fist, elbow or shoulder to initiate contact above the shoulders.

<u>DEFENSELESS PLAYER IS DEFINED</u> as a player, who, because of his physical position or focus or concentration, is especially vulnerable for injury.

<u>KICKOFF ALIGNMENT IS LIKE NCAA</u>. The kicker may be deeper, but teammates must be within 5 yards of the free kick line and 4 are required on each side of the kicker.

<u>FORCED TOUCHING ISN'T TOUCHING</u>. If a player is blocked into a loose ball, especially a kick, isn't new force and doesn't make the ball free or first touched.

<u>ALL DEFENSIVE PERSONAL FOULS ARE 15 ARDS AND AN AUTOMATIC 1ST DOWN</u>.

<u>STATE ASSOCIATIONS MAY REQUIRE GAME OFFICIALS</u> to take the field earlier than 30 min.

<u>TO EXTEND A PERIOD WITH AN UNTIMED DOWN</u>, time must expire during the down.

DYNAMIC FOOTBALL STATEMENTS

**A=offense, B=defense, K=kicking team,
R=receiving team the entire down**

DEFINITIONS:

The team that initiates the play can't go out of bounds and return.
Players shall not rough the kicker, holder, snapper or passer.
A block in the side is not a block in the back.
In the free blocking zone, A & B linemen may block each other below the waist.
In the free blocking zone, offensive linemen may clip or block Team B linemen below the waist, and A linemen may block any B player in the zone in the back.
The runner may be legally tripped, clipped and blocked in the back.
A swing and a miss is still considered to be a fight and is an ejection.
Force is blamed on the initiating team until the ball hits the ground.
How did the ball start moving-that's initial force!
A substitute can't be off-sides, but if he plays, it's illegal participation.
If a substitute enters and affects play during a down, it's illegal participation.
The line to gain and neutral zone are established on the ready for play.
On a simultaneous catch or recovery, give the ball to Team A or R.
A forward pass receiver must be eligible by both position and number.
Pass interference may occur only beyond the neutral zone.
Anyone may advance a fumble.
If Team B touches a pass, no pass interference is possible.

Batting is an intentional act; muffing is an unsuccessful or accidental attempt at possession.

Any ball in flight may be legally batted except Team A can't bat a backward pass forward.

KICKS:

A kick is a kick until it is possessed. The ball being touched or it bouncing doesn't end a kick.

After a kick is possessed, it is called a running play.

Team K shall not touch any kick it can't legally possess.

Team K shall not touch a kickoff before it hits the ground or an opponent.

Team K shall not block on kickoffs until it crosses R's restraining line, unless R touched it or R initiates the blocking.

Team K may NEVER advance a kickoff.

The only kick Team K may advance is a scrimmage kick in or behind their neutral zone, like a blocked punt.

Team K may bat a kick away from Team R's end zone to avoid a touchback.

Team R may fair catch any kick except for scrimmage kicks behind the line.

After a fair catch, Team A may kickoff from a tee for 3 points.

Kicks out of bounds are given to Team R.

Non-scoring kicks into Team R's end-zone are touchbacks.

Force is not a factor on kicks into Team R's end-zone. These are touchbacks.

Treat short field goals like a punt. Team R may advance & K might 1st touch.

If a field goal attempt is unsuccessful in the end-zone, it is a touchback.

SCORES:

Only the offense can score on an extra point (PAT).

The defense can't advance the ball on a PAT, it becomes dead immediately.

The tip of the ball across the goal line plane is a touchdown.

Team A must advance the ball completely out of their end-zone to avoid a safety.

ENFORCEMENT:

If a false start causes Team B/R to encroach, only penalize the false start.

PSK=Post Scrimmage Kick=Team R fouls 2+ yards down-field on a punt/FG until the kick ends, the foul is enforced from the end of the kick (beanbag spot).

To keep the ball, Team R/B must get it with clean hands to keep it, except PSK.

Enforce all non-player & unsportsmanlike fouls as dead ball fouls.

Enforce all dead ball fouls in order of occurrence.

"**All but one principal**"=penalize the offense from the spot that hurts them most, including fouls behind R's PSK spot, where the kick ended (beanbag lays).

OFFICIATING:

You only get one chance to make a first impression.

You're only as good as your last call.

Give the runner forward progress-he's earned it.

Be great dead ball officials.

Err on the side of safety, especially with player safety and lightning.

You can always pick up your flag.

Don't screw up scoring plays.

Call **ILLEGAL HELMET CONTACT** and actions on **DEFENSELESS** players.

Call the **ROUGH**, the **OBVIOUS**, the **CHEAP** and the **UNNECESSARY**.

Get the **FIRST** late hit and unsportsmanlike act. This sends a strong message.

If Team A/K's false start causes Team B/R to encroach, penalize the false start.

Become a master of your field position and the rules.

If you think you have a foul, you don't. Know you have a foul, except player safety fouls.

See everything you call, but don't call everything you see.

Don't look for fouls. Let them jump out at you.

Choose what you say wisely. It's never what you didn't say that gets you into trouble. It's always what you DO say.

Don't get out of shape. Stay athletic.

Don't officiate angry.

Control the game: don't dominate it.

The difference between a good official and a great official is the ability to concentrate the entire game.

What happens in front of you is more important than what you hear behind you.

During Referee-Coach disputes, your goal is to end the argument and move on to the next play.

USE THE PRESCRIBED MECHANICS FROM THE PRESCRIBED MANUAL!

SEE THE BALL!

HUSTLE!

This is a game, so HAVE FUN!

THE GAME, FIELD, PLAYERS & EQUIPMENT

Throughout this document:
Team A=snapped the ball, **Team B**=defense
Team K=kicked the ball, **Team R**=is trying to receive the kick
Officials are **R**= Referee, **U**=Umpire, **LM**=Linesman, **LJ**=Line judge, **B**=Back judge
To win the game, score the most points while preventing your opponents from scoring.

Playing the game

<u>TEAM A HAS 4 DOWNS</u> to advance the ball by carrying, passing or kicking it across the line to gain, usually 10 yards from the ball's position on 1st down. Points are made by touchdown, successful try, field goal or safety.

<u>THE GAME MUST BEGIN</u> with 11 players. Later, a team may play with less than 11, but the offense must snap with 7 linemen; if not, forfeit the game against the offense (1-0 or current score).

<u>THE OFFICIALS ASSUME AUTHORITY</u> 30 minutes before the game, or when they take the field by State Association directive. Their jurisdiction extends through the Referee's declaration that the game is over (holds the ball up). Incidents after the game is over can be addressed by State Associations. Prior to the game, the Referee meets with the head coach & captains to remind them that good sportsmanship is expected.

THE OFFICIALS make decisions on rule infractions, but may NOT use TV or replay equipment to make decisions. The Referee may rule on any situation not specifically stated in the rule book. This is a FINAL DECISION. The Referee's decision to forfeit a game is final.

NO PROTESTS ARE RECOGNIZED.

THE FIELD is 360' long by 160' wide.

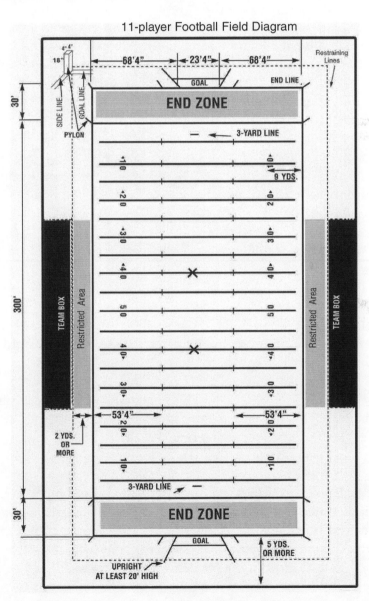

The field markings

YARD LINE MARKERS (usually orange or yellow triangles w/numbers) shall be soft, pliable construction and placed 5 yards from the sideline.

LINE COLOR is recommended to be white, but the goal lines & coaches areas should be different in color. Lines shall contain no lime or other caustic material, they'll mark every 5 yards. Aerosol paint is recommended. Yard lines stop at 4" from the sidelines, except for the goal lines (recommended to be different color than white) and end lines which touch the sideline. The sidelines and end-lines are out of bounds. All lines are to be clearly visible. If yard lines are placed near the sideline, the lines shall be 24" by 4" and stop 4" from the sideline.

NUMBERS ON THE FIELD are painted on every 10 yard line, 6' X 4', so the top of the number is 9 yards from the sideline. If an arrow is by these lines they point toward the nearer goal line. If no numbers are painted on the field, a 4" X 12" mini-hash will mark 9 yards from the sideline. All offensive players must come inside the numbers or this mini-hash to legally play after the ready for play (whistle).

YARD LINES mark all 98 yards, stop 4" from the sideline and are 24" tall X 4" wide.

CORPORATE ADVERTISING AND THE LOGO ON THE FIELD shall not interfere with the visibility of the required marks (ex. If there is a big eagle drawn at center field, the 50 yard line, hashes and 9 yard marks must be clearly visible.)

INBOUNDS LINES (HASH MARKS) The hash marks separate the field into thirds, 53' 4" each, and the marks are 24" long X 4" wide. The hash marks bisect the yard lines, making a "+". Pro or college hashes may be used if they are on the field.

2 YARD RESTRAINING BELT A 12" long X 4" wide with a 24" spaced broken or a solid line shall designate a 2 yard restraining belt around the field. This belt includes the coaches area and where the chain crew is to operate. This area is restricted. Media and non-team personnel aren't allowed inside the belt. At the snap, this area is empty.

TEAM BOX This is the area for subs, extra coaches, trainers & team personnel. It is 2 yards beyond the sideline & between the 25's. If both teams are on the same sideline, the team box is between the 20-45's.

COACHES' AREA is in front of the team box. 3 coaches are allowed between the team box & the sideline until the snap is imminent. At the snap, the coaches' area is to be clear. It is 2 yards tall. The coaches' area should have solid or diagonal lines of a non-white color. This area becomes a RESTRICTED AREA when the ball is about to become live.

END ZONE MARKINGS must stop 2 feet from the boundaries. Advertising & commercial markings are allowed in the end zone and on the field of play.

THE GOAL LINE is the inner edge of the line and is part of the end zone.

THE 3 YARD LINE is required to be marked and is 4" wide and at least 24" long.

PYLONS are 4" square X 18" high, red, orange or yellow, at the sideline & goal line, at the sideline & end line, and even with the hash mark & end line-these may be 3' off the end line, out of bounds. All pylons are in the end zone and are out of bounds.

THE GOAL is the area inside the goal posts. It is the vertical plane above the end line, inside the uprights, 23' 4" wide, above the cross bar, & 10' high at its top edge The uprights shall be at least 10' high, and pro/college uprights may be used if they can't be moved. The posts shall be no thicker than 4" and the only decoration is paint-white, silver or yellow, and a wind streamer 42" long X 4" wide that is red, orange or yellow. The lower stanchion(s) shall be padded at least up from the ground to 6" high.

Game equipment

THE BALL is pebble grained, tan colored cowhide or composition leather or rubber. It's weight shall be 14-15 ounces. The ball may have either 8 or 12 laces, with 1" white or yellow half stripe on the 2 panels with laces. The ball must be properly inflated to 12.5 to 13.5 pounds pressure and have the NFHS logo, but 8th grade and below may use a smaller ball. Each team provides at least one legal ball to be approved by the Referee before the game. Teams may request any ball to free kick or start a new series of downs (but not a "kicking ball" on 4th down). Officials change the ball on interceptions & kick returns for touchdowns and before the *point after touchdown* (PAT). Team A can't ask for a new ball after their touchdown for the PAT (no "kicking" ball).

A TEE made of pliable material, may raise the ball no more than 2" from the ground. Using an illegal (2+") tee is an unfair act, resulting in no PAT/field goal score.

THE CHAINS are 10 yards apart and usually have rods & a down marker. All rods must have flat lower ends covered by a protective cap. The chains & rods fix the line to gain. The down marker marks the spot of the ball & the number of the down. These are operated by the LM 6' off the sideline on the 2 yard restraining belt, opposite the press box. The crew may use unofficial chains & rods, or orange line to gain ground marker.

THE GAME CLOCK is provided by the game management, and the operator is approved by the Referee.

SUPPLEMENTARY EQUIPMENT, like a Referee microphone, must be approved by state associations.

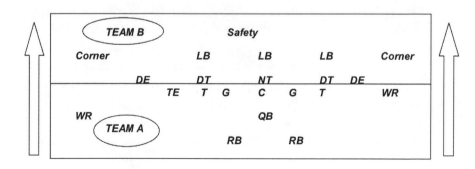

Player Designations

<u>CAPTAIN</u> One field captain communicates with officials. His first choice is final, except on a rare fair catch situation (see **"Awarded Fair Catch"**). He must decide on penalty options before any time-out is granted. Up to 4 captains may attend the coin toss.

<u>PLAYERS</u> wear jersey #1-99. Five offensive linemen must wear #50-79, unless on 4th down in scrimmage kick formation where everyone may have eligible numbers (on 1st, 2nd, and 3rd down scrimmage kick formations, 4 linemen must have ineligible numbers, thus making the A-11 offense illegal). On the field, no two teammates may wear identical numbers at the same time. Backs (QB, RB, WR) wearing #1-49 & 80-99 are eligible, by number to receive a forward pass if they are eligible by position. RB #61 may run the ball, but can't catch a forward pass.

MANDATORY PLAYER EQUIPMENT

Each player must properly wear these items.
They may not be altered to decrease protection.

<u>NOCSAE HELMET & FACE MASK</u> made from a material that won't chip. The helmet must display the external NOCSAE warning label about the risk of injury.

<u>AN ATTACHED 4 POINT CHIN STRAP</u> completely snapped.

<u>HIP PADS & BUTT (tailbone) PAD</u>

<u>JERSEY</u> that touches the pants, tucked if longer, with numbers 1-99. The numbers shall be approximately 1&1/2" wide, the same design on front and back, the jersey color can be the actual number with a boarder ¼" wide. The numbers shall be centered, at least 8" tall on the front, 10" tall on the back. The HOME TEAM wears dark jerseys, the VISITORS wear light.

<u>KNEE PADS</u> over the knees, under the <u>PANTS</u>. The knee pads shall be covered by the pants and the pants must cover the knees (the entire knee-cap).

ATHLETIC SHOES, if cleats, ½ inch or less long measured from the sole of the shoe to the tip of the cleat with a thickness of 3/8" to ½". The material must be non-chipping or nor develop a cutting edge. Screw-in or permanent cleats are legal, but no metal baseball style cleats are permitted. No gymnastic slippers, altered tennis shoes, ski or logger boots or shoes not intended for football.

SHOULDER PADS, they must be covered completely by the jersey.

THIGH GUARDS must be worn.

TOOTH & MOUTH GUARD, not completely clear or white in color, protecting the teeth with adequate thickness

NOTE: hip pads, knee pads & thigh guards must NOT be altered

OPTIONAL EQUIPMENT (approved by Umpire)

MEMORIAL PATCH must be State approved, 4" square in shape that doesn't interfere with the visibility of the jersey number.

AMERICAN FLAG 2" X 3" is allowed.

ATHLETIC GLOVES with NFHS/NCAA label/stamp or unaltered plain cloth gloves, without any web-like material between the fingers and/or thumb, completely covering the digits. They may be penalty flag colored.

HAND PADS & FOREARM PADS which will require the stamp/label in 2012 A hand pad has open fingers. Both may be anchored with athletic tape. They may be penalty flag colored.

BRACES, soft (cloth or neoprene), non-abrasive, non-hardening

ATHLETIC TAPE or support wrap, no more than 3 turns thick on the hand or forearm, to protect a existing injury

ARTIFICIAL LIMBS, DRUM on sideline for deaf snap count, & HEARING AID for deaf athletes, if state approved.

KNEE BRACE, under the pants. They do not need padding if they are un-altered from the manufacturer.

RIB PADS & BACK PADS, completely covered by the jersey throughout the game.

ONE SWEATBAND PER WRIST within 3" of thumb of a moisture absorbent material.

TOWELS, if worn, shall be any color except ball colored, may have a 2 ¼" manufacturers logo and teammates must wear the same color and design.

MEDIC ALERT TAG, taped but showing.

RELIGIOUS MEDAL, taped under clothes, not showing.

SHIN GUARDS meeting NOCSAE specifications

SHOULDER PAD ATTATCHMENTS like a shoulder brace that goes to mid-bicep, must be completely covered by the jersey.

SUBSTANCES LIKE RUBBER, LEATHER OR PLASTER in their final form that is hard on the hand, wrist, forearm (like a cast, wrist Velcro brace or finger splint) must be padded at least ½" on all exterior surfaces.

100% CLEAR EYE SHIELD, permitting clear vision of the eyes.

IF WORN, A PLAY CARD MUST BE WORN ON THE WRIST ONLY, not the waist.

ILLEGAL EQUIPMENT (umpire rules)

BALL COLORED helmet/patches/jersey/pads/towel/gloves.

TEAR-AWAY JERSEYS or jersey with knots, or sleeves with transverse stripes below the elbow.

HARD STUFF on the arm, hand, forearm, or elbow, including tin or wood or plastic. Casts and braces that are leather, plastic or plaster can be padded completely ½" to become legal.

SHIRTS that enhance contact with the ball.

SLIPPERY/STICKY SUBSTANCES on equipment, towels, uniform or body.

METAL on clothes, pads or person.

JEWLERY including cloth, string & rubber bands.

EYE SHIELDS that are tinted in any way, unmolded, or un-rigid eye shields.

UNIFORM ADORNMENTS, like "striping" the facemask or extra sweat or bicep bands. EYE-SHADE can only be one finger stroke and not extend to the cheek-bone. No writing or logo on eye-shade.

JERSEYS WITH MORE THAN one manufactures logo, larger than 2 & ¼" square or sizing info/washing label and no company reference, or with knots or tear-away jerseys.

COMPUTERS OR ELECTRONIC COMMUNICATION DEVICES No photographs, films, videos or internet replay or computer use for coaching purposes during a game. Cell phones and other communication devices may be used on the sidelines by anyone and players may use them outside the numbers during conferences.

THE HEAD COACH must verify to the Referee & Umpire that all players are legally equipped before the game. Any player equipment legality will be determined by the Umpire.

IF EQUIPMENT IS ILLEGAL OR MISSING, correct it prior to participation. If it becomes defective or illegal during use, an officials' timeout may be called to correct it on the field with teammate help (limited to :25 seconds).

EACH PLAYER shall properly wear mandatory equipment while the ball is alive: not having required equipment=**15 yds**; not properly wearing it during a down=**5 yds**.

COACHES MAY USE LAN phones, cell phones, walkie-talkies, headsets & audio cassette players. During time-outs, players and non-players may use this equipment between the numbers and sideline. No one may use other equipment, like film, video, computer, or TV, including during intermission.

COMMUNICATION DEVICES ARE ALLOWED for non-players and coaches. Players may use them during conferences outside the 9's. All devices are allowed during halftime intermission.

EACH STATE ASSOCIATION RULES ON THE FOLLOWING ITEMS:

Memorial patches
Size of the middle school ball and length of quarters
Playoff game ball
Equipment aiding game administration (Ref microphone)
Artificial limbs
Number of officials to be used in a game
Overtime procedure
Use of drum for snap count for hearing impaired
Mercy rule/running clock/point differential game termination
How to resume interrupted game
Length of halftime
Adding TV/radio time-outs
Time coin toss occurs
Size of the field for 6, 8 or 9 man football
The time officials are to take the field.

FOOTBALL DEFINITIONS

DEAD BALL The ball is not live, including the time between downs.

LIVE BALL A ball legally snapped or free kicked, and is in play until it's dead

LOOSE BALL is a ball not in possession-a pass, kick or fumble. If in flight, a loose ball may be caught or intercepted; if grounded, it may only be recovered. Momentum rules apply to all loose balls inside the 5 yard line.

BATTING INTENTIONALLY slapping or striking ball w/hand or arm.

BLOCKING is obstructing an opponent with use of the body.

IN ALL BLOCKING, NO locked hands; initial contact is below the opponent's shoulder; no one may throw or flip an elbow or move the forearm faster than the shoulder.

INITIAL CONTACT is to be above the waist (see **"free blocking zone"**) and below the shoulder, but a roll down block that started above then goes below the waist is legal if contact is maintained.

FRAME A blockers frame is in front of their body at or below the shoulders. The opponent's frame is their body, at or below the shoulders, including their side.

<u>CLOSED HAND TECHNIQUE</u> The elbows are inside or outside the frame; hands closed/cupped & not facing the opponent; forearms must stay close to the body, at a 45 degree or less angle.

<u>OPEN HAND TECHNIQUE</u> The hands extend beyond the elbow; inside the blockers frame (front of body at or below shoulder); inside opponent's frame (includes their side & front, at or below shoulder), unless he turns after the blocker commits. No blocking in the back, unless legal in the free blocking zone. The hands/palms face the opponent and his arms extend more than 45 degrees from his body.

<u>OFFENSIVE PLAYERS</u> The ball carrier MAY use his arm or hand to ward off a player, including using a hand on the facemask (not grasping). During kicks, offensive players may ward off blockers. During a loose ball/fumble, offensive players may push, pull, ward off an opponent as long as it isn't pass interference, a personal foul, or illegal use of the hands.

<u>DEFENSIVE PLAYERS</u> may ward off blocker w/unlocked hand/arm; may push, pull, ward off a blocker to get to ball carrier or loose ball, as long as it isn't pass interference, a personal foul, or illegal use of the hands. A player faking possession may be hit/held, but no unnecessary roughness is permitted.

<u>CONTACT BETWEEN PLAYERS</u> is to be at the shoulder or below, unless the opponent squats or ducks. If the opponent jumps, contact may occur below the waist.

<u>BLOCKING BELOW THE WAIST</u> is often illegal (see "**free blocking zone**"), initial contact occurs below the waist (including the hands) at the front or side, but this is LEGAL against the ball carrier. If the opponent is airborne, blocks below the waist are legal.

<u>CHOP BLOCK</u> (**illegal**) A combination high and low block. Low means the knees or below, high means above the knees. This is an illegal act, even in the free blocking zone.

INTERLOCKED BLOCKING (**illegal**) Grasping or encircling a teammate's arms or legs while blocking an opponent. This is often seen on a kick PAT-it's **illegal**.

THE KICKERS shall not block in the 10 yard neutral zone on a kickoff unless the block is initiated by the receivers.

CATCH is establishing player possession of a live ball in flight and MUST touch in bounds (1 foot) except for forward progress. Catching is after touching-if touching makes the ball dead, catching it doesn't matter. Simultaneous catch or recovery=joint possession by opponents, all in-bounds-give it to Team A or R or to the team last in possession. To complete a catch, possession must be maintained.

Ex. Airborne A89 secures the pass, but when he lands, the ball comes out. **NO CATCH.**

Ex. Airborne A89 secures a pass, would have landed in, but is pushed out by B4. **NO CATCH** *Ex. Airborne A89 secures a pass, his forward progress is stopped and he's carried out.* **CATCH**

CLIP (**illegal** except by Team A linemen in the free blocking zone) Initial contact is from behind & below the waist against a non ball-carrier.

BLOCK IN THE BACK Initial contact is INSIDE the shoulders, meaning hands are *on the numbers*. If in doubt, the block is LEGAL. If in doubt BLOCK IN BACK vs. CLIP-call a CLIP-but officials must see INITIAL contact to rule on clips & blocks in the back.

CONFERENCES (meaning coach with players) are OK after a PAT (extra point), field goal, safety, between the quarters & during timeouts. Conferences are to occur INSIDE the numbers with one coach in the huddle or OUTSIDE the numbers, with unlimited coaches and non-players. Authorized injury conferences are to occur OUTSIDE the numbers. Different types of conferences MAY be used during a game, but not both types during the same timeout. Communication devices are allowed by players outside the numbers.

FOOTBALL RULES: SIMPLY STATED 33

DOWN/LOSS OF DOWN Downs start with legal snaps or free kicks and end when the ball becomes dead. Loss of down means you can't replay it, due to offensive penalties, like fouls against the ball (illegal handing, forward pass, touching or intentional grounding).

ENCROACHMENT is any player illegally in neutral zone before the snap or free kick. The neutral zone is established on the Referee's ready for play (whistle). It remains until the legal snap or free kick. If a sub is on the wrong side of the neutral zone when the ball is snapped, he is an illegal sub. (NOT guilty of encroachment), but he better not play; if he participates actively in the play, this is **illegal participation**.

DO NOT CALL ENCROACHMENT until the center touches the ball, UNLESS Team B gives defensive signals in neutral zone or ANYONE touches an opponent before the snap or if the defense touches ball before the snap.

Ex. #1 Often a wide receiver will initially line up beyond the neutral zone. This is NOT encroachment, unless the center has his hand on the ball.

Ex. #2 When breaking the defensive huddle, B6 accidentally bumps the ball, this is ENCROACHMENT.

FAIR CATCH (FC)

ON A FREE KICK Team R may fair catch ANYWHERE.

ON A SCRIMMAGE KICK (punt or unsuccessful field goal) a fair catch may occur only beyond the neutral zone, since Team K may legally advance a kick in or behind neutral zone and advance for a 1st down. Team R signaling for a fair catch behind the line of scrimmage isn't a penalty, it just makes the ball become dead upon catch or recovery.

TEAM R If ANYONE signals validly or invalidly, NO one may advance the kick, and the signaler may not block until the kick ends. Team R may not advance once the signal is given. If player R4 signals and R5 makes the catch, it is not a fair catch but the ball becomes dead immediately.

AWARDED FAIR CATCH If an awarded fair catch is accepted, Team R's Captain may choose to snap the ball or try to kick the ball off a standard tee, with a 10 yard neutral zone, anywhere between the hashes for a field goal (3 pts). If Team K misses, Team R may advance. If a penalty occurs during the down after an awarded fair catch, the Captain's 1st choice options may be repeated. This is a rare exception to the captain's 1st decision on penalties (see "**Captain**").

VALID SIGNAL=arm extended and laterally waved at full arm length above the head by Team R is a valid signal. Any signaler is protected but may not block until the kick ends.

INVALID SIGNAL=it looks bad, or is made after Team R has touched the kick or the kick has touched the ground. (**5 yard PSK penalty,** see "**PSK**".)

ILLEGAL SIGNAL=the runner makes a fair catch signal after their catch or recovery. (**5 yard spot foul**).

KICK-CATCH INTERFERENCE results in an awarded FC or a 15 yard penalty.

FIELD AREAS

END ZONES are the 10 yards between end line & goal line-the goal line is in the end zone.

FIELD OF PLAY is the inbounds area, except for the end zones.

SIDE ZONES are the areas outside the inbounds lines (hash marks).

FIGHTING is an arm, hand, foot or leg, a swing and a hit OR miss by anyone in the game (**personal foul + ejection**).

1ST TOUCHING

FREE KICK/KICKOFF 1st touching is when Team K touches the kick in the 10 yd. neutral zone before Team R voluntarily touches it. This does not include a push or bat or muff into the kick caused by Team R.

SCRIMMAGE KICK (punt or missed field goal) Treat a missed FG like a punt. 1st touching may ONLY occur beyond the neutral zone, when Team K touches the kick before Team R, or Team K touches it at rest. Again, this is not caused by a push, block, muff or bat into the kick.

IT IS NOT 1st TOUCHING if Team K touches a scrimmage kick in or behind the neutral zone.

Ex. # 1 K4's punt hits snapper K8 in the helmet at the neutral zone. Team R can not choose to take the ball at that spot since it was in or behind the neutral zone.

Ex. #2 K4's punt hits rushing R10 in the helmet at the neutral zone. This does not make the kick a "free ball" since it was in or behind the neutral zone.

FORCE is a term meaning what made the ball go from the field of play into the end zone. Force matters only if the ball goes from the field of play INTO the end zone.

THE TEAM INITIATING PLAY IS BLAMED FOR FORCE INTO THE END ZONE UNTIL THE BALL HITS THE GROUND AND A NEW FORCE IS APPLIED.

INITIAL FORCE How did the ball start moving? That's initial force=a carry, an in flight fumble, an in flight snap, an in flight pass or any kick. If these balls are hit in flight, even if the change in direction is severe, force is blamed on the initiating team

Ex. #1 A punt is blocked by R9 out of K's end zone. Force is blamed on K because they kicked.

NEW FORCE is when the fumble, kick or backward pass has been grounded and some NEW action moves the ball into an end zone

Ex. #2 A punt is blocked by R9 & is grounded on K's 8 yard line. R9 muffs the ball into K's end zone where it goes across the end line. The force is blamed on Team R, resulting in a touchback. Yet, had R9 recovered the ball in K's end zone, touchdown.

EXCEPTION-there is no consideration of force on any kick going into R's end zone-this is always a TOUCHBACK and forced touching isn't touching.

Ex. #3 Trying to field the kickoff, the ball hits R6 and bounces across R's goal line. This kick will become dead immediately when it crosses the goal line, touchback.

Ex. #4 R12 muffs the punt at his 11. It rolls towards his end zone where K9 attempts to recover, but he muffs it across the goal line. This is still a kick across R's goal line, so it is a touchback.

BATTING a pass or fumble IN-FLIGHT is NOT new force-blame the force on Team A.

A MUFF of a grounded ball is ALWAYS new force, since the ball was already moving.

FORCE IS IMPORTANT in momentum rules (see "**momentum**").

FORMATIONS

SCRIMMAGE FORMATION (snap play) Team A must have 7 linemen on their line of scrimmage.

SCRIMMAGE KICK FORMATION is a traditional punt, field goal or PAT formation. No one may be under the snapper/center. If attempting to score by placekick, a holder must be in position to receive the snap, 7+ yards behind the line of scrimmage and the placekicker is within 3 yards of him. For punt formation, the punter is 10+ yards behind the line of scrimmage. In scrimmage kick formation on 1st, 2nd & 3rd down, the snapper may have a receivers number, but he can't be eligible and must be in between 4 other linemen who have ineligible numbers. There is no numbering requirement in this formation on 4th down, but interior linemen are ineligible by position to receive a forward pass if they are wearing #1-49 or 80-99. The numbering exception is intended for kicking downs.

FREE KICK FORMATION (kickoff) After the ready for play and until the kick, both teams must stay behind their free kick lines, but kicker & holder may be beyond. All Team K players must be within 5 yards of the free kick line, 4 on each side of the actual kicker who can be 5+ yards deep.

FORWARD PROGRESS the spot where the ball carrier (runner) advanced toward his opponent's end zone before being pushed back. If he's an airborne receiver, forward progress is the furthest spot he went toward his opponent's end zone when contacted by Team B. **GIVE THE RUNNER FORWARD PROGRESS-HE'S EARNED IT!**

FOULS & PENALTIES

FOUL A rule infraction for which a penalty is prescribed.
PENALTY The consequence against a team for committing a foul.

Types of fouls:

DEAD BALL occurs between downs and before the ball is legally snapped or kicked.

LIVE BALL occurs during a down

FLAGRANT Ejection offenses, including fighting, intentionally contacting an official, severe or extreme fouls putting an opponent at risk of injury, severe illegal helmet contact, acts with vulgar language or gestures, unsportsmanlike conduct and fouls with persistent or extreme conduct. **Penalty=15 yards + ejection.**

DOUDLE Both teams foul where the penalties offset. Double fouls do NOT include non-player (sub, coach, trainer) fouls or unsportsmanlike fouls or PSK fouls.

MULTIPLE 2+ fouls by the same team during the same down (except non-player & unsportsmanlikes) the opponent chooses which penalty to accept. Yet, if Team A scores and was offended, then is offended on the PAT too, both penalties can be administered.

Ex. A1 is face-masked during his touchdown run. A's Captain wants it administered on the kickoff. During the PAT, holder K4 is roughed. **BOTH penalties are administered**.

<u>NON-PLAYER or UNSPORTSMANLIKE</u> are NON-contact fouls that aren't illegal participation (by a sub) or don't influence the play in progress. These often occur in the team or coaches box by coaches/trainers/subs being inappropriate. *Note: if contact is involved (fighting) it is a personal foul, not an unsportsmanlike foul.*

<u>PLAYER</u> is a foul by a player on the field.

<u>PSK=POST SCRIMMAGE KICK</u> Team R fouls on THEIR SIDE of the expanded neutral zone (not counting illegal sub or illegal participation) before the kick ends (is caught, recovered or downed). PSK enforcement begins at the kick. **IF TEAM R FOULS 2+ YARDS BEYOND THEIR SCRIMMAGE LINE UNTIL THE KICK ENDS, THIS IS PSK!** PSK enforcement does not apply to a kick PAT or successful field goal.

<u>FOULS SIMULTANEOUS WITH THE SNAP</u> A violation occurs when the ball is snapped or free kicked (like an illegal shift/formation/sub/numbering).

<u>NO FOUL</u> is so bad that it causes loss of ball-but enforcement may cause a loss of down and award the opponents the ball.

<u>NO FOUL</u> causes the ball to become dead-play continues until the down ends unless the play is killed before the snap/kick.

<u>NOT A FOUL</u>, but has a penalty=1st touching, disqualified player, kick out of bounds (give it to Team R) and a forfeit (1-0 or current score).

FREE BLOCKING ZONE an area where legal clips, legal blocks below the waist & legal blocks in the back may occur. This zone is 8 yds. wide, 6 yds. tall square around the position of the snap.

<u>A PLAYER IS IN THE ZONE</u> if any part of his body is anywhere in the zone at the snap.

FOOTBALL RULES: SIMPLY STATED

<u>LEGAL BLOCK BELOW THE WAIST</u> Team A or B players on the line of scrimmage (Team B is on their line of scrimmage when within 1 yd. of line of scrimmage) block each other below the waist if the contact is in the zone before it disintegrates.

<u>LEGAL CLIP</u> Team A linemen against team B linemen only, contact is in the zone until the zone disintegrates. Team B may legally clip ONLY to get to ball carrier.

<u>LEGAL BLOCK IN BACK</u> by Team A linemen against Team B players in the zone at the snap. Team B may legally block in the back ONLY when going for the runner.

FREE BLOCKING ZONE RESTRICTIONS

WHO (until zone disintegrates):	*Against whom:*	*Not against whom:*
Team A linemen block below waist	Team B linemen	anyone else
Team B linemen block below waist	Team A linemen	anyone else
Team A linemen clip	Team B linemen	anyone else
Team A linemen block in back	Any B player in the zone	outside the zone

*Ex. #1 It is **legal** for nose tackle B7 to block the snapper below the waist at the snap.*

*Ex. #2 It is **legal** for guard A70 to let tackle B11 penetrate, then clip him.*

*Ex. #3 It is **legal** for tackle A64 to block blitzing linebacker B54 in the back.*

*Ex. #4 It is **illegal** for the snapper to block linebacker B17 below the waist up-field.*

*Ex. #5 It is **illegal** for fullback A34 to block defensive end B72 below the waist.*

THE ZONE IS GONE and these blocks become illegal when the ball leaves the free blocking zone (so we're talking like 1-3 seconds).

FUMBLE The loss of player possession except when handing, passing or legally kicking. An illegal kick is treated as a fumble.

HANDING is when possession changes from one player to another and the ball is in contact with both players. This is NOT a pass. Unsuccessful handing is a fumble.

FORWARD HANDING the entire ball is beyond yard line where the runner is positioned.

BACKWARD HANDING the ball is on or beyond the yard line where the runner is positioned.

ILLEGAL HELMET CONTACT 15 yard penalty and possible ejection

Butt blocking is a direct blow using the facemask, frontal area or top of the helmet as the primary point of attack (especially in line play). **This is illegal=15 yards**.

Face tackling is driving the facemask, frontal area or top of the helmet directly into the ball-carrier (instead of the hands or shoulder). **This is illegal=15 yds**.

Spearing is use of the helmet in an attempt to punish an opponent (especially on a defenseless or grounded player). **This is illegal=15 yds. + ejection**.

HITS ABOVE THE SHOULDERS MUST BE PENALIZED.

IF A HIT OR FOUL causes the helmet to come off, the player need not be replaced one down.

HUDDLE 2+ players of the same team together before a down. To legally participate, all Team A players must come within the numbers (9's) momentarily.

HURDLE **(personal foul, 15 yds.)** is Team A or B trying to leap over a standing opponent, with foot or knee first.

INTERCEPTION is catching an opponent's (in flight) fumble or pass. If the ball is grounded, this is called a recovery.

KICK INTENTIONALLY striking the ball with the knee, lower leg or foot.

THE KICK ENDS when ANY player gets possession or the kick is declared dead with no one in possession. **A KICK IS A KICK UNTIL IT IS POSSESSED!**

FREE KICK (like a kickoff) may be used after a safety or Team K may punt.

TEAM R may kickoff from a tee for 3 points after a fair catch or awarded fair catch

SCRIMMAGE KICK punt, drop kick or place kick (off a 2" tee with a holder) in or behind the neutral zone.

SCORING ATTEMPTS BY KICK must come from the ground (not by a punt).

KICKOFF A kickoff begins each half, occurs after field goals & after PATs. Kickoffs must be by drop kick or place kick, but a punt may occur for a free kick after a safety.

DROP KICK (very rare) the kicker drops the ball & kicks it just as it bounces or hits the ground. A drop kick may be used for any kickoff from a tee for 3 points fair catch scoring attempt, a PAT, a field goal (like Doug Flutie for the Chargers in January, 2006) a kickoff, a scrimmage kick or after a safety.

PLACE KICK The ball is in a fixed position on a tee or a holder controls the ball. The footing can't be improved with a towel, etc. Place kicks may occur during scrimmage kicks (A.K.A. field goal or PAT), a kickoff, after a safety and on a kickoff from a tee for 3 points after a fair catch or awarded fair catch.

PUNT ball is dropped and kicked before it hits the ground. Team K may punt after a safety.

ILLEGAL KICK (**15 yd. penalty**) When an illegal occurs, the loose ball maintains its status.

LINE OF SCRIMMAGE It's established on the ready for play whistle. On a scrimmage play (snap) it's the vertical plane through the tip of the ball closest to each team.

TEAM A IS ON THEIR LINE OF SCRIMMAGE (is a lineman) when they are facing their opponent's end zone, shoulders approximately parallel to line of scrimmage, with the head or foot even with the snapper's waist.

TEAM B IS ON THEIR LINE OF SCRIMMAGE when they are within 1 yard of line of scrimmage at snap. If in the free blocking zone, defensive linemen may be blocked below the waist, blocked in the back or may be legally clipped until the zone is gone.

LINES

BOUNDARY The end lines & sidelines are out of bounds.

END LINE is the line underneath the goal posts, all the way to the sidelines.

GOAL LINE The vertical plane toward the field of play, is entirely in the end zone. It includes beyond the sideline plane if a runner is touching inbounds. Team A's goal line is behind them. It should be a different color than regular field lines.

INBOUNDS LINES (hash marks) cut the field into 1/3rds. The yard line bisects (makes a "+") the hash mark. All snaps and free kicks must occur within the hash marks.

LINE TO GAIN The yard line established on the ready for play when a new series (1st down) is awarded. It's usually 10 yards in advance of the front of ball, or is the goal line.

SIDELINE The outer limit of field of play & end zones, the line are out of bounds.

YARD LINE 1-50 from goal line to mid-field. If the yard lines (dashes) are marked near the sidelines, they stop 4" from sideline and are 24" tall.

A 2 YARD RESTRAINING BELT will surround the field, with a solid line or broken 12" line with 24" breaks. This area includes the coaches area and where the chains will be set. No other persons are allowed in this 2 yard belt.

MUFF The touch or accidental kick of a loose ball in an unsuccessful attempt to possess it.

NEUTRAL ZONE is the space between free kick lines (10 yds.) or 11" (size of ball) on scrimmage plays. The neutral zone is established when ball is marked ready for play.

EXPANDED NEUTRAL ZONE The neutral zone expands up to 2 yards toward Team B/R's goal line during downs. This is an issue on pass plays, field goal & PAT plays (Team A blockers may block forward up to 2 yards and any touching of a kick in the expanded zone is ignored). The expanded neutral zone does NOT expand into the end zone.

OUT OF BOUNDS A player is out when they are on or outside a boundary line.

THE RUNNER is out when THEY touch out. If they touch a player or an official who is out, they are NOT out of bounds.

A LOOSE BALL is out when it touches ANYTHING OUT.

PARTICIPATION is any act or action by a player or non-player that influences a play.

PASSING is throwing a ball from possession. It travels in flight.

A FORWARD PASS is thrown with its initial direction toward the opponent's end zone. If the QB is hit in the act of throwing (his arm was moving forward)=forward pass. A forward pass is thrown beyond the neutral zone when the ENTIRE ball is BEYOND the neutral zone. A forward pass ends when it is caught, it hits ground or is out of bounds. Team A may throw only 1 forward pass per down.

BACKWARD PASS The initial direction is parallel or toward a team's own end line. It ends when it is caught (in flight), is recovered (grounded) or is out of bounds.

PLAYER DESIGNATIONS There are **only 22 players** at any given time, the 11 Team A/K players and the 11 Team B/R players on the field.

Team A=the team that snaps the ball=offense.
Team B=the defensive team during scrimmage plays.
Team K=the team that legally kicks the ball.
Team R=the team that attempts to receive a kick.
A1, K4, B3, R9 are members of their respective teams. These designations do NOT change during a down. If B9 intercepts, still call him B9 though he is advancing the ball. See "TARGETING" for defenseless player definition.

BACKS are non-linemen for Team A. The QB is a back and can break the waist of the snapper, but other backs can't break the waistline of the lineman nearest them or the waist of the snapper.

OFFENSIVE BLOCKER Team A players blocking or in a position to block.

A CAPTAIN is designated in the pre-game/overtime tosses; during 2nd half options; makes foul/penalty decisions; and may request ball location between the hashes for a PAT, safety, kickoff, touchback, fair catch & during overtime.

A DISQUALIFIED PLAYER can't participate further-if he does=**illegal participation**.

HOLDER is the player that holds the ball for a kick. He gets some protection on kicks.

KICKER is the player who touches a ball with their foot or lower leg in a legal punt, place kick or drop kick. Until the lower leg or foot touches the ball, he's a runner. He remains a kicker until he regains balance; advances 5 yards on a kickoff; or the kick touches the ground or any player. Once the ball hits his toe, he has protection. A ball blocked/touched near the punter may admit some contact by the player who touched/ blocked the kick.

LINEMAN is a Team A player on his line of scrimmage, facing Team B's goal line with shoulders roughly parallel to the line, & his foot or head breaks the snappers waist at the snap. Team B players within one yard of the line when the ball is snapped are linemen.

NON-PLAYERS include anyone from a team that isn't on the field participating. Coaches, subs and trainers are non-players, including subs on wrong side of neutral zone at the snap. If an illegal sub enters during a down=**illegal participation.**

A LEGAL FORWARD PASSER is protected until the pass ends or until he moves to participate in the play. AN ILLEGAL PASSER is not protected, but B shall not commit personal fouls against him. A backward passer is not protected either. To be considered the passer for roughing calls, he must throw a legal forward pass.

REPLACED PLAYERS must initiate their exit from the field within 3 seconds of being replaced. (see "**SUBSTITUTE**") He must exit his sideline and immediately head toward his team box.

RUNNER=BALL CARRIER or a player pretending to be the runner may be tackled.

SNAPPER=CENTER is a lineman. He is protected from direct contact on scrimmage kick formation plays until he may regain his balance, blocks or participates in the play.

A SUBSTITUTE=SUB replaces a player or fills a vacancy. He becomes a player and replaces a player when he indicates to a team mate "I got you", enters a huddle, is in formation, or participates during a down. That former player must initiate his exit within 3 seconds. A sub is not called a player until he is on his side of neutral zone. If ball is snapped and he is on the wrong side of the neutral zone, this is an **illegal substitution**, not encroachment. Subs may not enter during a down=**illegal participation**.

PLAYS FOR PENALTY ENFORCEMENT

LOOSE BALL PLAYS are kicks (except for special PSK enforcement having Team R foul on their side of expended neutral zone), LEGAL forward passes, backward passes, a snap and fumble behind the neutral zone and ALL runs before these kicks, legal forward passes, snaps, fumbles or backward passes.

A RUNNING PLAY is advancing the ball with possession. There may be several runs during a play. The end of this document will discuss enforcement on these plays-see "**SPOTS**" to help understand enforcement for each type of play.

POSSESSION

PLAYER POSSESSION The ball is held or controlled by a player by it being snapped, handed to him or by catching or recovering a loose ball.

TEAM POSSESSION occurs during player possession and remains when the ball is loose. A live ball is ALWAYS in team possession-in possession of the team who LAST had it.

CHANGE OF POSSESSION occurs when the opponent gains player possession during a down.

READY FOR PLAY is the Referee's whistle signaling the ball is to be snapped or free kicked within 25 seconds. This also establishes the neutral zone & line to gain.

RECOVERY is gaining possession of a GROUNDED ball (fumble, backward pass or kick that bounces). If a player is airborne, they complete the recovery when they contact inbounds with possession. If two opponents simultaneously recover (both inbounds, possession at the same time) give the ball to Team A or R or, if multiple changes in possession on the same play, give it to the team last in possession. Recovering a loose ball inside the 5 yard line is a momentum exception. (see "MOMENTUM").

<u>RULE</u> is a regulation that governs the game. Some rules are stated, some are assumed (ex. no face masking; OK to fake a punt). Unless stated in a play, assume the ball is live & no foul has occurred. If there is a foul, it isn't a double foul or multiple foul, unless it's stated.

<u>SCRIMMAGE</u> is a play that starts with a snap.

<u>SHIFT</u> One or more Team A players that set, then move and reset into a new position. After multiple players move (even breaking the huddle), all must stop 1 second before the ball may be legally snapped. Also, after all are still one second, one player may go into motion.

<u>SNAP</u> is legally passing or handing the ball backward off the ground to initiate play. The snapper/center may adjust the ball (sideway roll) but afterward he can't move the ball or remove both hands until the snap or a whistle. The snap is a quick, continuous movement backward-the ball must immediately leave the hand of the snapper and touch a back (QB or other back) or the ground before it may be touched by a line player (so the old "center sneak" playground play is **illegal**).

<u>SPOTS</u>

<u>THE BASIC SPOT</u> is a general reference for penalty enforcement.

Loose ball play-the Basic Spot is where the ball was last snapped=the previous spot.

Running play-the Basic Spot is where the run ends (tackle, spot of fumble/beanbag spot).

<u>ENFORCEMENT SPOT</u> is the spot where penalties are enforced

DEAD BALL SPOT is the front point of ball when it became dead. **Exception**: when the ball is coming out of Team A's end zone-the ENTIRE ball must get out to avoid a safety.

INBOUNDS SPOT is the spot on the hash mark where ball is placed. It is even with the place the ball went out of bounds or became dead in the side zone.

OUT OF BOUNDS SPOT is where the front of the ball went out of bounds.

PSK=POST SCRIMMAGE KICK SPOT The back judge bean bags where the kick ends on a punt or missed field goal. The PSK spot is where Team R caught or recovered the kick or where it's awarded to R from Team K's 1st touching. If Team R commits a penalty on their side of the expanded neutral zone in these two situations, the penalty is enforced from the PSK spot or the "all but one" spot (see pg. 55).

PREVIOUS SPOT is where the ball was last snapped or free kicked.

SPOT OF THE FOUL is where the foul occurred-sometimes where the flag is thrown.

RUN ENDS SPOT is the spot where the ball became dead by rule, by tackle, the knee down, out of bounds or where the runner lost possession (fumble). The spot of momentum recovery is the spot of the catch or recovery inside the 5 yard line on change of possession plays (beanbag spot).

SUCCEEDING SPOT is spot where we were supposed to snap or free kick but a foul occurred. Dead ball fouls have succeeding spot enforcement.

TACKLING is a defensive player holding the runner until his forward progress is stopped or by bringing a runner down. Face tackling is **illegal helmet contact.**

HORSE-COLLAR TACKLE is **a personal foul (15 yds.)** and occurs when the tackler grasps the inside back or side of the collar or jersey or shoulders and subsequently pulls the runner down backward.

TEAM DESIGNATIONS

OFFENSE=TEAM A
DEFENSE=TEAM B
TEAM R=receiving a kick
TEAM K=kicking team
Team designations DO NOT CHANGE during a down.

**TOUCHING** is contacting the ball by touching it or being touched by it. A ball touching an inbounds official is ignored and remains alive.

**TRIPPING** is use of the lower leg or foot to hit an opponent below the knee. It is **legal** to TRIP the runner/ball carrier.

**TARGETING IS DEFINED** as taking aim with the helmet, forearm, hand, fist, elbow or shoulder to initiate contact above the shoulders.

**DEFENSELESS PLAYER IS DEFINED** as a player, who, because of his physical position or focus or concentration, is especially vulnerable for injury.

PERIODS, TIMING & SUBS

Timing of periods

<u>4 QUARTERS</u>, 12 minutes each. *JV* may play 10 or 12 min. quarters.
<u>MIDDLE SCHOOL</u> (no 9th graders) 8 min. quarters

<u>1 MINUTE</u> between quarters 1&2, 3&4

<u>HALFTIME</u> is determined by each state association, between 10 & 20 minutes. The 3 minute warm-up period begins immediately following of the half-time period. The head coach is responsible for having his team on the field for the mandatory warm-up time.

<u>OVERTIME</u> is determined by each state association, often the Kansas City Tie-Breaker.

<u>KANSAS CITY TIE-BREAKER</u> is NOT sudden death; both teams get a chance on offense from the 10 yard line (unless moved by penalty) to score a field goal, touchdown and PAT. Each overtime series is 1st & goal. At the end of the 4th quarter, teams are sent to their box for 3 minutes. All 2nd half timeouts do NOT carry over. Each team gets one timeout per overtime period. The visitors still call the toss and choose to be Team A, Team B or which end of field to play. The Team A captain may request ball placement each overtime series between the hashes. If Team A scores a touchdown, they get a PAT. Their opponents get the same opportunity at the same goal. It's OK to attempt a field goal on any down. If Team B intercepts/ recovers a fumble, or gets possession-that overtime series is over-kill it! After both teams have an opportunity to be Team A and the score is still tied, they are sent to their sidelines for 2 minutes-bring out the captains again-the loser of the last toss gets the first choice-Team A, Team B or end of field. If Team A strangely scores a safety on their series (RARE-like if they fumble on the 2 and Team B forces the grounded fumble into their own end zone where B recovers) Team A gets 2 points and their opponents still get a chance to score, 1st & goal, and they better score, or they lose. Team A gets a new 1st and goal (series) if a roughing penalty occurs or if during a field goal, Team R touches the kick beyond the expanded neutral zone but before the end zone and then Team K recovers. If Team B somehow scores a touchdown or safety the game is over. If the PAT isn't needed, don't play it *(ex. Home team fails to score in their series then Visitors score a touchdown in theirs, game over, no PAT)*.

MERCY RULE is determined by each state association. It may result in game termination at a certain point differential or running clock in the 1st or 2nd half.

SHORTEN PERIOD A period may be shortened in an emergency only if agreed upon by both coaches & Referee-if all 3 agree, the game may also be terminated.

INTERRUPTED GAMES are considered by each state association. If it resumes, the same score, down & distance, position, time remaining, etc . . . the game resume from the point of interruption.

WEATHER CONCERNS if conditions are considered hazardous to life & limb of participants, the officiating crew suspends the game and will not resume until BOTH game administrators & the Referee agree to play-err on the side of safety here!!!

Starting the half/period

A KICKOFF starts each half.

COIN TOSS When it is held is determined by each state association. Up to 4 captains may attend the toss; one is designated as the speaking captain; the Visitors call the toss, calling "heads" or "tails" before the actual toss; the winner chooses to take the option now or defer his option until the 2nd half; options are to receive, kick or defend a goal—the loser has the remaining option. During the toss, teams are restricted to their team box or an area well away from the toss. Non-Captains may not come out to the hashes or numbers (9's). Teams can't send 5+ Captains (Unsportsmanlike for either offense.)

<u>AT THE END OF THE 1st & 3rd QUARTER</u> change ends of the field. Team A will have the same ball position, down & distance, and line to gain toward the other goal.

Ending period/half

<u>IF THERE IS NO VISIBLE CLOCK</u>, with 4 minutes to go in 2nd & 4th quarters, an official's timeout is called to tell the coaches & captains the time remaining.

<u>WHEN THE CLOCK GOES TO 0:00</u> play continues until the down is over. A horn may sound, but should be turned off if possible.

<u>HOLD AN UNTIMED DOWN</u> if, on the last timed down of a period and time expires during that down, a player foul is accepted, (except unsportsmanlike, non-player, loss of down foul or succeeding spot enforcement), a double foul occurs, an inadvertent whistle occurs or a touchdown occurs. If a defensive penalty occurs during a successful PAT or field goal and the scoring team wants the succeeding spot enforcement, end the period and enforce that penalty on the kickoff to start the next quarter. Also, if a penalty results in a safety during the last timed down of a period, do NOT extend the quarter.

<u>OFFICIAL END OF A PERIOD</u> After hesitating to see if there was a foul, a timing error, or if a coach-referee conference is desired, the Referee holds the ball above their head to indicate official end of the period (after this, it's too late to question the last play or fix a timing error). If a dead ball foul or unsportsmanlike foul or non-player foul occurs after time expires, enforce the penalty from the succeeding spot after changing direction. If altercations occur after a game is ended, State Associations may intervene.

STARTING THE CLOCK

Situation	*the clock starts*
Kickoff	when legally touched.
Start of quarter	when legally snapped
After a change of possession	on the snap (or see kickoff)
After a legal kick	on the snap (or see kickoff)
Fouls	depends on the play-either on the snap or the ready
Inadvertent whistle	on the ready
After a called time-out	on the snap (or see kickoff)
After an officials' time-out	depends on the play-either the on snap or the ready

Don't run the clock during a PAT, during overtime or during untimed downs.

SITUATIONS & CLOCK STATUS

Stop clock on	*when*	*clock resumes*
Foul	end of play	depends on last play
B gets ball	end of play	snap
R gets ball	end of play	snap
After a legal kick	end of play	if new series is awarded, snap
Touchdown/touchback	end of play	snap
Out of bounds	end of play	snap
Incomplete forward pass	end of play	snap
Timeout	when player or head coach calls	snap
Period ends	end of play	snap/touch on kickoff
Delay of game	end of :25 sec. clock	snap
Consuming time illegally	end of play (delay of game)	snap
Official's timeout	end of play	depends on last play
Scores	by rule, upon score	touch on kickoff

Fair catch	catch, recovery or awarded FC	snap
The clock doesn't start on K's 1st touching of a free kick.		
Helmet comes off	if runner, immediately, if not, at the end of play	depends

THE REFEREE MAY CORRECT obvious timing errors up to two plays later, unless the period ends. He may also order the clock started/stopped is a team is illegally consuming/conserving time.

Timeouts

3 CHARGED TIMEOUTS per half. Only the head coach or his designee and players may request a time-out. A Head Coach in the press box IS allowed to designate an assistant to have this right. Any unused time-outs do NOT carry into overtime.

NO TIMEOUT is granted until the captain makes penalty decisions.

CHARGE A TIMEOUT IF MORE THAN 25 SECONDS is required to fix equipment on the field or send him off as an injury.

ON A COACH REFEREE CONFERENCE with no change in the Referee's ruling, the charged time-out remains charged. It may last longer than one minute to resolve the dispute. An authorized coach-player conference is permissible during coach-referee conferences either inside or outside the numbers (9's).

A CHARGED TIMEOUT lasts 1 minute, but may be shortened if BOTH teams are ready to play. Two time-outs in a row is OK. The officials shall notify the captain & coach when they are out of time-outs.

WHEN A TEAM IS OUT OF TIMEOUTS, don't give them another one unless they point out "Look Ref, he's hurt," to fix player equipment, and a coach may call an extra timeout to request a coach-Referee conference, but he better be right-if not, the Referee enforces a **delay of game penalty** and may do what he wants with the clock.

ON-FIELD EQUIPMENT PROBLEMS If equipment may be repaired, a :25 second officials time-out may be called to fix the problematic equipment with the help on his fellow on-field players (no sideline help-if he needs sideline help, he has to leave for one play). A difficult chin strap is covered here, but for a badly torn jersey, he has to leave.

THE REFEREE DECLARES AN OFFICIAL'S TIMEOUT FOR:

Measurements	@ 4 minutes if no visible clock (2nd & 4th quarter)
1st downs	On-field equipment problems (:25 seconds)
Water breaks	Referee changes ruling after conference with coach
Fouls	Delay in making the ball ready for play
TV/radio timeouts	To dry/change ball, unless done efficiently
Injuries	Changes of possession
Helmet comes off	The 1 min. after a PAT, field goal, or safety & between quarters

AN AUTHORIZED CONFERENCE (coach speaking to players on the field) may only occur during charged, TV/radio timeouts, water breaks, and the one minute after a PAT/field goal/safety. Two types of conferences may occur, but ONLY ONE may be used each timeout. One coach may go inside the numbers (9's) and speak to 11 players or everyone may be outside the numbers (9's) to talk. Headsets, cell phones and other communication devices may be used during a sideline conference.

INJURIES If an official stops the clock for a suspected injury, the player must leave for one timed play unless there is halftime or overtime. *HELMET COMES OFF* not caused by a foul=injury. *BLEEDING or blood on the uniform*=injury. If an authorized conference is allowed during an injury, it shall occur outside the numbers.

CONCUSSIONS If it is determined by the game official that a player is showing signs of a concussion, is out for rest of the game approved to return by an appropriate health-care professional. *SIGNS OF A CONCUSSION* include dizziness, headache, confusion, balance problems, and loss of consciousness. He must be replaced for at least one down.

A COACH-REFEREE CONFERENCE occurs outside the numbers (9's) with the wing official. Initially charge that team with a timeout. The head coach may only discuss the misinterpretation/ misapplication of a rule (not judgment) on the play that JUST HAPPENED. If a period is officially over, it's too late for a conference. If the decision remains unchanged, the timeout remains charged. If the ruling is changed, this becomes an official's timeout, the other coach is notified, and the clock status depends on the last play.

Ready for play

AFTER THE READY Team A/K has 25 seconds to snap or kickoff. If not . . .

DELAY OF GAME:

Not snapping/kicking within 25 seconds

Unnecessarily carrying the ball after it's declared dead

Not un-piling

No change in coach-Ref conference & no team timeout left

Snapping/kicking before the ready

Any conduct that unduly prolongs the game

Not properly wearing required equipment just before snap (like a mouthpiece hanging out)

THE REFEREE MAY ORDER THE CLOCK stopped or started if a team is attempting to conserve/consume time illegally.

UPON ORDER, a team must play within two minutes to avoid a forfeit (1-0 or current score).

GAME MANAGEMENT is responsible to make the end zones (for halftime warm-up) and field available so each half of the game will begin on time.

Subs

NO SUB may enter during a down=**illegal participation**.

UNLIMITED SUBS are allowed between downs.

REPLACED PLAYERS must leave within three seconds after being replaced (**or illegal sub**); they must exit their side of the field and immediately go to their team box (**if not, dead ball foul**).

NO SUB may enter & withdrawal or exit & return, unless there is an accepted penalty, dead ball foul, timeout or a period ends.

ILLEGAL SUBSTITUTION=replaced player or sub doesn't get off the field (behind wing official) before a down begins. This also includes a Team A player not reporting inside the numbers or mini-hash after the ready for play.

IF AN ILLEGAL SUB PLAYS=**illegal participation & a 15 yard penalty.**

SUBS are required to be on their side of neutral zone to be considered players. If not, they are called subs and better not influence the play (**illegal participation**). This sub IS NOT offside or guilty of encroachment.

ILLEGAL SUB PENALTY=**5 yards**, previous spot, unless they enter during the down=**illegal participation.**

BALL IN PLAY, DEAD BALL & OUT OF BOUNDS

Starting a play

<u>A KICKOFF</u> resumes play after a field goal, PAT and starts each half.

<u>A FREE KICK</u> occurs after a safety (K may punt or kickoff from the 20 yard line). A free kick may also occur after a fair catch/awarded fair catch. Though rare, Team R's Captain may ask to free kick from a tee for 3 points at a point between the hashes on the yard line of the fair catch. A 10 yard neutral zone is established and if the placekick goes through the uprights, this is a 3 point goal. If a foul occurs during the down (snap or free kick) after the fair catch, the Team A/R captain may still choose to "kick for 3 from a tee." This is a rare exception to the captain being able to change his mind on a penalty option.

<u>SNAPS</u> occur on scrimmage plays. Snaps must be between the hashes and the ball remains alive until it's declared dead.

<u>THE BALL REMAINS DEAD</u> if these snaps or kicks occur before the ready for play, if the snap or kick is illegal or if another dead ball infraction occurs.

Dead ball and the down ends

<u>DEAD BALL FOULS ARE DEAD BALL FOULS</u>! Blow the whistle to indicate there was a foul before the snap of free kick.

THE BALL IS DEAD & THE DOWN IS ENDED WHEN

Helmet comes off the runner
Runner goes out of bounds
Runners forward progress is stopped
Field goal/PAT touches K inside R's end zone
Fair catch is caught/recovered by R
Simultaneous catch or recovery occurs
Any score occurs
A live ball goes out of bounds
Team B gets the ball on a PAT
K possesses a free kick
Team K recovers any kickoff anywhere
An inadvertent whistle is blown
Team K's PAT is no good
Loose ball is motionless-no one grabs it

The ball touches something weird (inadvertent whistle coverage)
Legal/illegal forward pass is incomplete
R gives a valid or invalid fair catch signal and then possesses a kick
Any legal non-scoring kick breaks Team R's goal line plane
Field goal/PAT crosses R's goal line and is no good
Anything but runner's hand or foot hits the ground
Team K downs or possesses scrimmage kick beyond the neutral zone
Scrimmage kick comes to rest beyond the neutral zone
If a kick PAT or FG hits Team R or an official in the end zone and goes through uprights (good)

EXCEPTION: The place kick holder in scrimmage kick formation may rise to catch or recover an errant snap and *immediately* return to their knee to place the ball or again rise to run or pass.

AN INADVERTENT WHISTLE prematurely ends a down. Inadvertent whistle options are not given if a penalty is accepted for a foul which occurred during the down. But if there is no foul (or a foul is declined) and an inadvertent whistle is blown . . .

REPLAY THE DOWN, AT THE PREVIOUS SPOT if it occurred during a legal forward pass, snap in flight or during legal kicks (meaning the ball hasn't yet been possessed).

IF THE BALL IS LOOSE from a fumble, backward pass, illegal forward pass or illegal kick, the team LAST IN POSSESSION may take the ball at the spot where possession was lost or they may choose to replay the down from the previous spot.

IF IN PLAYER POSSESSION, the team in possession may take the ball at the spot where the ball was when the whistle was blown or replay the down from the previous spot.

Out of bounds & inbounds spot

A LOOSE BALL is out where the front of the ball crossed the sideline plane when it went out. Bring it to the hash mark equal to that spot.

A FORWARD PASS out of bounds goes back to the previous spot.

A BALL OUT BEHIND THE GOAL LINE is a touchback, safety or field goal/PAT.

THE PYLON is out of bounds, but completely in the end zone.

PLAY A kickoff bounces at the 3 yard line and hits the pylon. Ruling=touchback.

A RUNNER IS OUT when he touches out. The ball is placed inside the hash mark equal to where the front of ball was when he touched out, not where his foot touched out.

THE DEAD BALL SPOT is where the next play will resume, except for incomplete forward passes where the ball goes back to previous spot.

A BALL DEAD IN SIDE ZONE is brought to the near hash, unless it is an incomplete forward pass (previous spot) or inadvertent whistle with a chosen replay (previous spot).

THE PENALTY ENFORCEMENT SPOT may overrule a dead ball spot.

PLAY A11 runs for 20 yards and is declared dead in the side-zone. There was a hold in the center of the field at the line of scrimmage. Ruling=enforce from the center of the field.

TEAM A OR K MAY DESIGNATE THE SPOT TO SNAP OR KICK INSIDE THE HASHES ON:

PATS	FREE KICKS (after safety)
FAIR CATCH	AWARDED FAIR CATCH
KICKOFF	TOUCHBACK
STARTING EACH OVERTIME	

If a dead ball foul or replay of down occurs during these situations, the captain may re-indicate the spot they want to initiate play.

SERIES OF DOWNS, NUMBER OF DOWN & TEAM POSSESSION AFTER PENALTY

Series of downs

<u>SERIES OF DOWNS</u> Team A gets 4 downs to advance across their line to gain. 1st downs start a new series unless replaying 1st down.

<u>TEAM A IS AWARDED A 1st DOWN</u> when, by virtue of their advance and after considering their live ball penalties, they've crossed their line to gain. If a dead ball foul occurs by Team A after the play (a teammate's late hit), lift the chains, administer the penalty and have a new 1st & 10 and new line to gain after marking off their foul. Team A earns a 1st down when, by the virtue of their *live ball* acts, they cross their line to gain.

<u>ON 4TH DOWN ONLY</u>, non-player, unsportsmanlike and dead ball fouls can not be considered in awarding Team A a 1st down. These will be administered at the succeeding spot.

Ex. 4th & 8 on the 50. A28 advances to the B's 45 (is 3 yards short) and B49 taunts. A's series is over, B's penalty is administered, B's ball, 1st & 10 on the B30.

AWARD A NEW SERIES IF NEW SERIES IS AWARDED TO:

Team A has ball beyond the line to gain	Team A, 1st & 10 or goal
Team B has the ball at the end of a down	Team B, 1st & 10 or goal
Team A has the ball after 4th down behind the line to gain	Team B, 1st & 10 or goal
Change of possession (***see below)	who has it at end of the down, 1st
K's scrimmage kick is recovered by R	Team R, 1st & 10 or goal
K's scrimmage kick-joint recovery	Team R, 1st & 10 or goal
K's scrimmage kick goes out of bounds (even on 3rd down)	Team R, 1st & 10 or goal
No one recovers/downs K's scrimmage kick	Team R, 1st & 10 or goal
A free kick is recovered beyond the neutral zone	who gets it, keeps it, 1st & 10
R touches the kick beyond expanded neutral zone	who gets it, keeps it, 1st
R touches a kickoff before it goes out of bounds	Team R @ spot, 1st & 10 or goal
K 1st touches scrimmage kick beyond neutral zone	Team R at the spot of their advance or spot of 1st touching

*****CHANGE OF POSSESSION PLAYS, except for PSK (see ENFORCEMENT)***

<u>IF THE TEAM IN FINAL POSSESSION</u> got the ball legally (A.K.A. "clean hands" or no foul), they may keep the ball, 1st down.

<u>IF THEIR OPPONENT FOULED</u> before the change of possession, they must decline that penalty to keep the ball (*ex. Team A has an illegal formation at the snap and throws an interception-Team B must decline the penalty to keep the ball*).

<u>IF A CHANGE OF POSSESSION OCCURS</u> and the team in final possession got the ball illegally (A.K.A. "dirty hands" or cheating), and the penalty is accepted, the ball is given back to Team A (*ex. Team B commits pass interference and intercepts-give the ball back to Team A since*

Team B had "dirty hands" when they possessed the ball). PSK is an exception to the "clean hands" rule.

SCRIMMAGE KICKS

<u>IF TEAM K</u> recovers a scrimmage kick (punt, blocked field goal) in or behind their neutral zone they may advance, but the down counts-so they better cross the line to gain.

<u>IF TEAM R</u> touches the kick *beyond* the expanded neutral zone and it goes back behind the neutral zone, Team K may (but doesn't have to) advance and will get a 1st down. Team R's touching a kick beyond the expanded neutral zone makes this a free ball and a new series will be awarded to the team in possession at the end of the down.

<u>THE SPOT OF 1st TOUCHING</u> disappears if Team R later touches the kick then commit a fouls or if the penalty for a foul during the down is accepted.

<u>IF TEAM R</u> touches the kick *down field and Team K recovers*, it is Team K's ball, but since this is still a kick, Team K can't advance.

<u>**TEAM K MAY NOT ADVANCE ANY KICK EXCEPT**</u> for a scrimmage kick *behind* their line of scrimmage.

<u>**A KICK IS A KICK UNTIL IT'S POSSESSED**</u>, so K can't advance a down field kick.

<u>PSK</u>=Post scrimmage kick. This is the spot where a scrimmage kick (punt, short FG) ended by it being possessed or downed. A beanbag is dropped at this spot. If Team R committed a foul 2+ yards down field toward their goal line from the line of scrimmage, they can keep the change of possession with "dirty hands" but their penalty will be enforced from the bean bag or "all but one" enforcement spot.

FREE KICKS

ACTION DURING A FREE KICK AWARD A NEW SERIES TO:

R touches a free kick & it goes out of bounds	Team R, 1st down at spot on hash
Kick is recovered beyond the 10 yard neutral zone	whoever possesses it, 1st down
Joint possession of any free kick	R, 1st & 10
K possesses the kick inside 10 yd neutral zone– no voluntary R touch	R, spot of 1st touching, 1st down

<u>TEAM K</u> can't block until the ball crosses R's restraining line unless they can legally possess it, unless the receivers initiate the block in the neutral zone.

Note: On 1st touching by Team K during a free kick, the ball remains alive but the clock doesn't start until it's touched by any player outside the neutral zone. Team R may take the ball at that spot, even if they recover and advance, as long as they don't foul during the run or accept any foul.

DOWN & POSSESSION AFTER A PENALTY

<u>IF A PENALTY IS DECLINED FOR A FOUL</u>, play the next down.

<u>IF THERE'S A DOUBLE FOUL</u> (Team A & B commit live ball fouls with no change of possession) replay the down.

<u>AFTER A DISTANCE PENALTY</u> The team in possession at the time of the foul keeps possession, but they may turn the ball over if they don't get a 1st down after 4th down and with penalty enforcement.

Ex. 4th & 6 from the 50. Team A throws a forward pass from B's 48. It's still A's ball, but after penalty enforcement for the illegal forward pass, B gets the ball on A's 47.

<u>FOUL DURING A SCRIMMAGE DOWN</u> The ball is given back to Team A, unless there was a change of possession and the foul was after the

turnover; or if Team R is first to touch a kick beyond the neutral zone, in which case whoever gets it, keeps it.

ON A DOWN WITH AN ACCEPTED FOUL, replay the same number down again, unless the penalty includes an automatic 1st down, a loss of down or the ball is beyond the line to gain after enforcement. If there is a change of possession, with a loss of down penalty, the loss of down aspect is ignored, only the yardage is marked off. If Team A is well beyond the line to gain and commits a loss of town foul, the loss of down aspect is also ignored, only the yardage is assessed.

DEAD BALL FOUL Enforce the penalty and play the next down unless Team A gets a 1st down from the penalty yardage.

FOUL SIMULTANEOUS WITH THE SNAP (like formation/numbering/shift) Enforce the penalty then replay that down, unless the yardage gives Team A, 1st down.

FOUL BEFORE A FREE KICK-(like an illegal sub or Team K encroachment) Enforce and kick.

FOUL DURING A FREE KICK (until the kick ends=possession) Have Team K re-kick unless Team R has the right to maintain possession by rule (like a kick out of bounds, R may take it at the spot or 25 yards downfield from the spot of the kick, which is usually the 35). If a foul occurs from the moment the kicker's toe hits the ball until it is possessed, these are LOOSE BALL FOULS, and the ball shall be re-kicked after penalty enforcement. **NOTE, this is NOT PSK,** because it isn't a punt or short FG. Loose ball Team R or K fouls have previous spot enforcement.

Ex. #1 Team K kicks off from their 40. While the kickoff is in flight, at the R45, K3 blocks below the waist. Team R advances to the R28. RULING: If the penalty is accepted, it is enforced from the spot of the kickoff because the ball was loose when the foul occurred, re-kick.

Ex. #2 Team K kicks off from their 40. While the kickoff is in flight, R47 holds at the 50. R advances to the R28. RULING: If the penalty is accepted, loose ball foul, enforce from the K40, re-kick.

AFTER A FOUL, A SERIES ENDS WHEN:

The penalty awards an automatic 1st down.
Declining any penalty leaves Team A behind the line to gain after 4th down.
Accepting or declining any penalty leaves Team A beyond the line to gain.
Declining any penalty leaves Team B in possession.
A foul after a change of possession is accepted or declined.
Team R touches a scrimmage kick beyond the neutral zone, unless a penalty is accepted for a foul that occurred before the kick ends that isn't PSK enforcement.
Team A commits a loss of down foul on 4th down & enforcement leaves Team A behind the line to gain

<u>WHEN A SERIES ENDS</u>, award a new series, 1st & 10 or goal, unless it's after a scoring play (PAT & field goal, then kickoff) or after a fair catch or awarded fair catch (since Team R's Captain may choose to "kickoff for 3 from a tee").

The line to gain & measurements

<u>THE LINE TO GAIN</u> is 10 yards in advance of the front of the ball on a first down or is the goal line.

After the Referee signals 1st down, all fouls, including non-player and unsportsmanlike fouls that occur AFTER that signal and BEFORE the ready for play whistle, mark off the penalty first, THEN set the chains, 1st & 10 and blow the ready for play. After the ready is blown and a foul occurs, mark off dead ball fouls but LEAVE the chains. The only way to have 1st & 25, 1st & 15, or 1st & 5 is for the Referee to have established the line to gain by blowing the ready for play whistle. If then someone violates a rule (non-player, false start) that penalty gets marked off and the possibility of 1st and longer/shorter than 10 exists.

Ex. #1 Team A makes a 17 yard gain to get a first down. The Referee signals 1st down and the chains are lifted. The runner gets up and showboats. **Flag-unsportsmanlike. Back Team A up 15 yards, then set the chains 1st & 10 and blow the ready.**

Ex. #2 *Team A gains 17 yards, the Ref signals 1ˢᵗ down. The chains are set, the ready for play is blown, THEN the runner taunts an opponent.* **Back them up 15 yards, but don't move the chains (the whistle was blown). Team A now has 1ˢᵗ & 25.**

<u>MEASUREMENTS</u> may be requested by Captains, but the Referee may deny the request if it is obvious to them the ball is short (or beyond). During a measurement, leave the ball where it became dead (even if on a sideline or in the side zone). The Linesman (LM) brings the chain into the field and places it on the solid 5 or 10 yard line in between the two rods of the chains. The Line Judge (LJ) shows the LM the spot on that yard line that is parallel to the ball. The Back Judge (BJ) holds the ball still. The Umpire (U) stretches the chain after everyone is ready and the Referee (R) rules 1ˢᵗ down or short-and indicates this to the press box. If the ball touches the rod, it's a 1ˢᵗ down. If it's short in a side zone, the R grabs the chain link in front of the ball and tells the LJ, LM & U to bring the chains to the near hash mark and re-sets the ball on the hash mark.

<u>WHEN STARTING A NEW SERIES</u>, the back of the ball becomes the front of the ball on changes of possession. On incomplete pass plays on 4ᵗʰ down, put the ball back exactly the way it was before the snap-so the back of the ball is now the front of the ball. This requires the chains to be moved 11 inches toward the goal line of the team who just turned the ball over.

<u>AFTER A SAFETY/ TOUCHBACK</u> place the ball with its nose on the 20.

<u>THE BALL TOUCHING THE GOAL LINE PLANE</u> is a touchdown, safety or touchback. Team A, when pinned deep, must get the ball COMPLETELY out of their own end zone to avoid a safety.

KICKING & FAIR CATCH

Kickoffs & free kicks

<u>DURING KICKOFFS, THE NEUTRAL ZONE</u> is ALWAYS 10 yards wide. Usually, Team K's free kick line is the 40 and Team R's free kick line is the 50.

<u>AFTER A SAFETY</u>, K's free kick line is the 20, R's line is the 30. Team K may punt within 1 yard of the free kick line or kickoff from the 20.

<u>AFTER A FAIR CATCH OR AWARDED FAIR CATCH</u> K's free kick line is where the ball was caught or awarded if they want to kickoff from a tee for 3, but they usually snap instead.

<u>FREE KICKS</u> occur between the hashes. Once the spot is designated, it can't be changed. Team K must have at least 4 players on each side of the kicker, within 5 yards of the free kick line and only the actual kicker can be 5+ yards deep.

<u>AFTER THE WHISTLE</u>, no one may encroach except the kicker and holder.

<u>TEAM R</u> may recover & advance any kick, unless a fair catch signal was given.

<u>TEAM K</u> may recover (recover=the ball has it the ground) a kickoff if it goes 10 yards beyond their free kick line & has hit the ground or an opponent (unless Team R's touch or muff is caused by K's block-this

69

touching is not considered in giving Team K the right to recover & retain possession). Team K may keep a ball if it goes 10 yards & touches the ground or opponent, but may not advance. **A kick is a kick until it's possessed!** Team K can't advance a muffed kick. Once Team R catches or recovers a kick, the kick is over and their advance is called a running play. If Team R were to then fumble, Team K could recover and advance since the kick ended upon possession.

<u>TEAM K CAN'T LEGALLY BLOCK</u> until the ball crosses R's restraining line unless R initiates the block. Team K can legally block in the neutral zone if R has touched the kick an it's in the neutral zone.

<u>JOINT POSSESSION/RECOVERY OF A KICK</u>, the ball is given to Team R.

<u>A KICKOFF OUT OF BOUNDS</u> is Team R's ball. If untouched by Team R, the penalty options are to take the ball where it went out, re-kick after a 5 yard previous spot penalty or take the ball 25 yards beyond Team K's free kick line (usually the 35 yard line).

<u>IF A KICK BECOMES DEAD</u> with no one in possession, give the ball to Team R.

<u>1st TOUCHING</u> When Team K touches the kickoff (intentionally or accidentally) without Team R causing this contact inside the 10 yard neutral zone, this is called 1st touching. A bean bag is thrown at this spot. The clock does not start and the play is not over. Team R may then recover and advance, but can still choose to take the ball at the spot of 1st touching unless there is an accepted foul during the play.

<u>DO NOT REPEAT A FREE KICK</u> unless a foul occurs during the kick and taking the penalty requires a re-kick; a double foul occurs; or an inadvertent whistle occurs during the kick. Again, a kick ends when possession is gained.

<u>A KICKOFF OUT OF BOUNDS UNTOUCHED BY TEAM R</u> (between the goal lines): **penalty:** options are to re-kick with a 5 yard penalty, R may decline the penalty & take the ball at the out of bounds spot (this often occurs on failed on-sides kick); or Team R may take the ball 25 yards beyond the free kick line (usually at the 35 yard line).

IF TEAM R TOUCHES THE FREE KICK and it goes out, they get it at that spot.

Scrimmage kick (which is a PAT, punt or field goal)

TEAM K may punt, place kick, or drop kick, in or behind the neutral zone on any down.

TEAM R may catch or recover a scrimmage kick (except PAT) in the field of play and advance unless there was a fair catch signal. If Team R recovers the kick in K's end zone=touchdown. Forced touching is not touching.

TEAM K may catch, recover & ADVANCE a scrimmage kick in or behind the neutral zone, but beyond the neutral zone, if R hasn't touched it, this is 1st touching. If Team R touches the scrimmage kick beyond the neutral zone, Team K may recover & keep possession, but this is still a kick and Team K can't advance because it is beyond the neutral zone. Team K & R's touching is ignored if caused by an opponent's block, bat or muff. Also, Team K may not obstruct R's path to an in-flight kick, but if there is no R player near an in-flight scrimmage kick downfield, K can catch the kick and not be guilty of kick-catching interference. Forced touching is not touching.

TOUCHING A LOW SCRIMMAGE KICK is ignored in or behind the neutral zone (if it hits the snapper in the helmet or the rusher attempting to block it). This touching isn't 1st touching or a touch that makes it a "free ball" that Team K could keep. Team K linemen may go down field immediately after the snap.

THE NEUTRAL ZONE MAY NOT BE EXPANDED into the end zone.

SCRIMMAGE KICK OUT OF BOUNDS, give the ball to Team R.

JOINT POSSESSION OF A SCRIMMAGE KICK, give the ball to Team R.

Touchback

ON A FIELD GOAL/PAT the kick is not dead as it crosses the goal line, unless it is obvious the kick attempt will fail, or does fail in the end zone, resulting in a touchback.

OTHER SCRIMMAGE KICKS (or free kicks) that cross R's goal line are touchbacks.

FORCE IS NOT A FACTOR ON KICKS ENTERING TEAM R'S END ZONE These are

ALWAYS touchbacks. If any kick is touched in the field of play then crosses Team R's goal line, this is still a touchback, even if the touch causes significant movement of the kick toward Team R's goal line.

IF A PAT/FIELD GOAL hits a Team R player in the end zone, let the play continue. If the ball hits R4 then caroms through the uprights, the scoring attempt is good. If Team K touches the kick in the end zone, touchback.

Fair catch

ANY TEAM R PLAYER may signal for a fair catch while any kick is in flight. The signaler(s) is protected from contact, but he can't block until the kick ends. R7 may signal for a fair catch, but it is NOT a fair catch if R2 catches the kick. It is not a fair catch if the signaler catches the kick behind the neutral zone on a scrimmage kick, since Team K could legally catch/recover and advance.

IT'S NOT A FAIR CATCH, but kill the play if: player R4 signals fair catch and player R1 catches the kick; the signal is invalid (looks bad); or if Team R catches a kick after a signal behind the neutral zone. In these situations, there is no penalty, but Team A may not request to "kick from a tee for 3" nor may they designate the spot between the hashes to initiate the series since this isn't a fair catch-it's just a dead ball.

ON A FAIR CATCH OR AWARDED FAIR CATCH the offended team may spot the ball between the hashes to start a new series or they may "kickoff for 3 from a tee" with a 10 yard neutral zone but if this kick goes through the uprights, it's a 3 point field goal. If this kick is short, Team R may advance. If the kick is no good or enters the end zone, it's a touchback for Team R.

NO R PLAYER shall advance if a signal has been given by any Team R player.

TEAM R SHALL NOT make an invalid signal (looks bad or signal after the kick hits the ground). This is a **PSK enforcement**. The runner shall not, after possessing the kick, make an illegal signal (since the kick is over, this signal is illegal) **5 yard spot foul**.

KICK CATCHING INTERFERENCE

ON A FREE KICK IN FLIGHT, Team K can't legally possess it, so they shall not interfere with Team R's right to catch the kick. Team K has no right to the kick until the kick touches the ground and goes 10 yards or touches an opponent.

ON A SCRIMMAGE KICK Team K can't legally touch the kick beyond the neutral zone (unless Team R has touched the kick) so they shall not interfere with Team R's right to catch it in flight. Yet, if no one of Team R is in position to make such catch, Team K may run underneath the kick and catch it legally. It's a dead ball there, give it to Team R. Team K may also try to prevent a touchback by batting the kick away from Team R's end zone.

***PENALTY FOR KICK CATCHING INTERFERENCE* 15 yard spot foul or take an awarded fair catch at the spot of the interference.**

SNAPPING, HANDING & PASSING THE BALL

Before the snap

SNAPPER RESTRICTIONS

The snapper MAY....	*The snapper CAN'T....*
Have his head in the neutral zone	Have his feet or body in the neutral zone
Roll the ball left or right in adjustment	Turn the ball end to end (180 degrees)
Have a hand on the tip of the ball	Have his off-hand in the neutral zone
Keep ball roughly parallel to the sideline	Hold the ball crooked or parallel to the goal line
Slowly take one hand off ball or ground	Remove both hands from the ball
Must pause after initial adjustment	Make a false snap move
He may roll it left or right	He may NOT move the ball's position forward

PENALTY=dead ball 5 yard illegal snap.

<u>NO PLAYER</u> may touch the ball (except snapper) or touch an opponent. Team B can't give defensive signals in the neutral zone. **PENALTY=encroachment 5 yard foul.**

ENCROACHMENT There is NO ENCROACHMENT CALLED until the center touches the ball. Once the snapper's hand(s) touches the ball, no one Team A or B may encroach the neutral zone.

PENALTY=encroachment 5 yard dead ball foul (but use preventative officiating here).

FALSE START Team A shall not false start after the ready for play by making a fake charge or abrupt shift that simulates a snap. No offensive interior lineman may remove his hand from the ground once it is down (except the snapper). ANY ACT CLEARLY intended to make Team B encroach is a FALSE START. *Ex. On punts, Team K linemen jerk down or shout to make the defense jump off side is a false start.* **PENALTY= 5 yard, dead ball foul.**

IF A FALSE START MAKES TEAM B/R ENCROACH, CALL ONLY FALSE START!

Position, numbering & action at the snap

AFTER READY FOR PLAY & BEFORE THE SNAP all Team A players must come inside the numbers or mini-hash. Penalty=**illegal. sub, 5 yds, previous spot.**

THE SNAPPER & GUARDS may lock legs (like an" X") but no other linemen may. **Penalty=illegal formation, 5 yds. previous spot.** Every other lineman must have their feet outside the feet of the player next to them.

TEAM A PLAYERS may stand, kneel or crouch, but can't lie down (**illegal participation**). At the snap, Team A must have 7 players on the line of scrimmage.

BACKS may not break the waistline of the nearest lineman (**illegal positioning**).

THE QB must have his hands in position to receive the snap if the ball is indeed snapped between the center's legs, but the QB is not required to receive the snap. He can't line up under the guard to deceive the opponents. **(illegal positioning).**

ON A SNAP the ball must immediately leave the snapper's hands. It must touch the ground or a back before it touches a Team A lineman (**illegal snap, 5 yards, dead ball foul**).

THE SNAPPER & TEAM A LINEMEN can't receive a handoff unless they turn completely backward and come back one yard behind the line of scrimmage then receive the handoff. After a snap, putting the ball on the snapper's (or other linemen's) back is **illegal forward handing, 5 yards, loss of down.**

NUMBERING REQUIREMENT Team A must have 5 offensive linemen #50-79 on their line of scrimmage, except during scrimmage kick formation (no QB and someone is 7+(placekick) or 10+ (punt) yards back to receive snap) because there is no numbering requirement (since special teams players are often receivers & defensive backs) on 4th down only. On 1st, 2nd and 3rd downs, if Team A shifts into scrimmage kick formation, the snapper may have a receivers number, but the 4 linemen next to him must have ineligible numbers. On 4th down only, there is no numbering requirement. Even though #84 may line up as a guard on 4th down in scrimmage kick formations, he is not eligible to catch a forward pass or go down field if a forward pass crosses the expanded neutral zone. These rules make the California A-11 offense illegal on 1st, 2nd and 3rd downs.

IN SCRIMMAGE KICK FORMATION, the snapper is protected from a direct charge until he has time to snap & recover. (**roughing the snapper, 15 yards + 1st down**)

NO TWO PLAYERS may wear the same number on the field at the same time (**illegal numbering**).

SHIFT Before a play, all 11 Team A players must stop for 1 second before the snap. After that 1 second, one player may go into motion parallel to the line of scrimmage or toward his end line **(illegal shift or motion).** Linemen and the player who lined up under center, if any go in motion, they are to be at least 5 yards behind the line of scrimmage at the snap unless they re-set as a back.

FUMBLEROOSKI is only legal if the Referee is notified before that play. Team A may snap the ball and intentionally fumble it, but a player on his line of scrimmage can't advance a planned loose ball.

Handing the ball

<u>BACKWARD HANDING</u> by any player is legal anytime.

<u>FORWARD HANDING</u> is only legal in or behind the neutral zone, to any back, or end, if both players are behind the neutral zone. But this handing can not be to an end who lined up adjacent to the center. *PLAY Overload right, left guard is the end. He can't receive the handoff unless he makes the 180 degree turn and is a yard off the line of scrimmage.*

<u>LINEMEN</u> may only receive handoffs after they turn a full 180 degrees around AND after are he is one yard behind the line of scrimmage. This order doesn't matter, but both must occur before an offensive lineman receives a handoff. Thus, the old playground "snap & hand it to the guard or center" play is **illegal**.

<u>AFTER A CHANGE OF POSSESSION</u>, no forward handoffs are legal. **(5 yards, spot foul, no loss of down since it was during a change of possession)**.

Fumble & backward pass

<u>BACKWARD PASS</u> Any runner may backward pass at any time. If for some reason no player attempts to gain possession of a fumble or backward pass (after a long delay), it's given back to the team last in possession at that dead ball spot. This could result in a touchdown, touchback or safety, even without possession.

<u>A FUMBLE</u> is when a player loses possession.

<u>ADVANCEMENT</u> Fumbles or backward passes may be recovered (after it hits the ground), caught or intercepted (in flight) and advanced by any player during any down.

Ex. Runner A28 fumbles at the 50 to the B47 yard line where A32 recovers and advances to the 30. **Legal play, even on 4ᵗʰ down.**

<u>OUT OF BOUNDS</u> If a fumble or backward pass goes out of bounds between the goal lines or becomes dead in bounds with no player in possession or in joint possession, the ball is given back to the passing or fumbling team, unless they fumbled or backward passed it out of bounds behind the line to gain after 4ᵗʰ down.

<u>A FUMBLE THAT GOES FORWARD</u> then out of bounds is marked where it crossed the sideline. If this forward fumble is intentional, this is an **illegal forward pass, spot foul, 5 yards, loss of down.**

<u>TOUCHBACK/SAFETY</u> If the ball is fumbled or backward passed out of bounds in the end zone, the ball is **given to the team defending that goal**. If the same team forced the ball from the field of play into their own end zone, this is a safety. If their opponents forced the ball from the field of play into that end zone, it is a touchback.

**Famous example: In a Dallas Cowboy's game a player named Lett recovered a ball and went over 80 yards toward the opponent's end zone for an apparent score. This was a big guy, so around the 7 yard line he was slowing, but decided to "high step" into the end zone. He didn't know a Bill's receiver was behind him. The Bill's player slapped the ball out of Lett's hand, across the goal line and out of bounds across the end line. The ball was given to Buffalo, 1ˢᵗ & 10 on the 20. Even though the Bill's player hit the ball hard, force is blamed on the player carrying the ball, so the result of the play was a touchback.

Forward pass

<u>LEGAL FORWARD PASS</u> Team A throws the ball forward with both feet of the passer in or behind the neutral zone when the ball is released. Only one forward pass from behind the neutral zone is legal.

<u>ILLEGAL FORWARD PASS</u> is a pass made from beyond the neutral zone; a pass intentionally grounded into an area with no eligible offensive receiver around; or a pass intentionally thrown incomplete to conserve

time or to avoid a sack (QB has no protection in any of these situations) or is a forward pass after a change of possession. The QB is not given protection on any illegal pass. A ball thrown on the track or into the stands is usually **illegal**.

LEGAL GROUNDING (usually late in a half) After a direct hand to hand snap, the QB may legally throw a forward pass immediately to the ground to stop the clock.

ILLEGAL FORWARD PASS PENALTY Illegal forward pass plays are treated like running plays: the enforcement spot is the spot of the illegal pass. Even if the penalty is declined, the down counts and the succeeding spot is where the ball was thrown-or Team B may accept the result of the play (like if Team B intercepted).

ANY FORWARD PASS CAUGHT may be advanced by Team A or B.

SIMULTANEOUS CATCHES are dead immediately. Give the ball to the passing team.

INCOMPLETE FORWARD PASS is when the forward pass touches the ground, goes out of bounds, when an airborne player gets possession and lands out (but if he touches an out of bounds player or official and if he still touches in, it's a catch) or touches anything else out of bounds (like a crossbar or pylon). Count that down, unless there is a change of possession. The next down is at the previous spot.

ELIGIBILITY applies to legal forward passes. Both ends, all backs, the QB and all Team B players are eligible by position (17 players at the snap) but Team A players must wear #'s 1-49 or 80-99 to be eligible to receive a forward pass. Position alone doesn't make a player eligible. Number alone doesn't make a player eligible. Both are required. On 4th down scrimmage kicks, there are likely many players with good numbers, but are in ineligible positions. Once a player starts a down eligible, he remains eligible throughout the down.

IF TEAM B touches a pass, every Team A player becomes eligible.

ELIGIBILITY REMAINS THROUGHOUT A DOWN. If a wide receiver goes out of bounds, he remains eligible even though a penalty may be involved.

PASS INTERFERENCE may only occur BEYOND THE NEUTRAL ZONE on LEGAL forward passes. If the pass is touched by Team B, no pass interference is possible.

PASS INTERFERENCE RESTRICTIONS BEGIN FOR:

TEAM A at the snap.

TEAM B when the ball leaves the passer's hand. Defenders may contact (A.K.A. "chuck") potential receivers until the receiver is even with the defender (because receivers are considered blockers) until the pass is thrown. Once the ball leaves the passer's hand, Team B's downfield contact or "chucking" is no longer legal.

PASS INTERFERENCE RESTRICTIONS END for

TEAM A when Team B touches a legal forward pass
TEAM B when the pass is touched by ANYONE

INELIGIBLE TEAM A PLAYERS (like linemen) only become eligible when Team B touches the pass. If a Team A ineligible touches the pass, the ineligibles remain ineligible. Team A linemen touching this pass is illegal touching anywhere on the field, including a tight end who was covered up by a wide receiver or an interior lineman intentionally touching a pass he can't legally possess.

ILLEGAL TOUCHING If an ineligible Team A player INTENTIONALLY touches a legal forward pass anywhere before touching by Team B, this is illegal touching. This includes a wide-out or tight end who is "covered up" by a wide receiver on the end of the line. **PENALTY=5 yards, loss of down.** If the illegal touching is well beyond the line, previous spot enforcement, but the illegal touching is near or behind the neutral zone, spot foul. A pass hitting the snapper in the back is NOT illegal touching.

<u>INELIGIBLE A</u> players may NOT touch a legal forward pass until it touches Team B.

IT IS PASS INTERFERENCE IF:

***Any player beyond the neutral zone interferes with an eligible opponent's opportunity to move toward, catch or bat a legal forward pass.

***A player "face guards" or obstructs a player's vision as the pass arrives without attempting to catch, intercept or bat the pass, *even if no contact is made.*

<u>PENALTY FOR PASS INTERFERENCE BY TEAM A</u>=**15 yards, previous spot.**

<u>PENALTY FOR PASS INTERFERENCE BY TEAM B</u>=**15 yards, previous spot.**

<u>PASS INTERFERENCE (A or B)</u> is enforced from **the previous spot**.

IT IS NOT PASS INTERFERENCE

***If unavoidable contact occurs when 2 eligible receivers make a bona fide attempt to catch/bat a pass, like if they are both looking back for the pass and their feet get tangled up.

***If Team A's contact on Team B's linesman is immediate and doesn't go beyond the expanded neutral zone.

***Contact by a defender obviously away from the direction of the pass is not considered pass interference. This could be holding or illegal use of the hands or a personal foul, but not pass interference.

PASS INTERFERENCE CAN'T OCCUR BEHIND THE NEUTRAL ZONE.

SCORING PLAYS & TOUCHBACK

TOUCHDOWN=6 points.   *FIELD GOAL=3 points.*   *SAFETY=2 points.*

PAT=1 points if field goal or 2 points for touchdown

SAFETY ON A PAT=1 point. This is rare: Team A, after their touchdown, decides to go for 2. During their run, A4 fumbles the ball. After it hits the ground, B6 muffs the ball, forcing it into their own end zone where it is possessed by B, goes out of bounds or is declared dead. Since they forced it into their own end zone, it is a safety, but only 1 point.

FORFEITED GAME score is 1-0, unless the offended team is winning, then it is the current score.

ONLY THE OFFENSE CAN SCORE on a PAT.

Touchdown

POSSESSION OF A LIVE BALL IN THE OPPONENT'S END ZONE IS ALWAYS A TOUCHDOWN!

IT IS ALSO A TOUCHDOWN WHEN

***A runner advances the ball from the field of play & penetrates the imaginary plane of the opponent's goal line (just the tip across the goal line plane is a touchdown).

***Any player recovers or catches a loose ball in the opponent's end zone, including over the goal line before landing with the ball.

***When a backward pass or fumble is declared dead in the opponent's end zone with no player in possession.

Ex. Team A fumbles on Team B's 3 yard line, the ball goes into Team B's end zone, but no one tries to recover. After it is still (like 5 seconds+) then the officials may award a touchdown to Team A.

NOTE: If an inadvertent whistle is involved in this example, it is not a touchdown-give the ball back to Team A at the spot of the fumble or replay the down, using the procedures for an inadvertent whistle.

<u>DEAD BALL, NON-PLAYER OR UNSPORTSMANLIKE FOULS ON A TOUCHDOWN</u> Both teams have the option of enforcing the penalty on the PAT or putting it onto the kickoff

PLAY A11 is running for an 85 yard touchdown. The Team A coaches enter the restricted belt or field and an official contacts the coach and a flag is thrown. Ruling=the touchdown counts and Team B may choose for the PAT to occur at the 18 or have Team A kickoff from the 25.

PLAY A11 scores a touchdown. After the score, B6 is profane toward the official. Ruling=Team A may play the PAT from the 1.5 yard line or kickoff from Team R's 45.

<u>ON CHANGE OF POSSESSION TOUCHDOWN PLAYS</u> (Team B scores and Team A fouls after the turnover), enforce Team A's post-possession fouls on the PAT or on the kickoff. If Team A fouled before the change of possession, Team B must decline that penalty to keep the score.

PAT

<u>AFTER A TOUCHDOWN</u>, the scoring team snaps anywhere between the hashes on the 3 yard line to score a 2 point touchdown or a 1 point field goal. Do not have a PAT if a touchdown ends the game and the extra point won't change the outcome. Only the offense can score on a PAT.

THE PAT IS OVER IF:

Team B gets possession The ball becomes dead for any other reason
The kick attempt will fail The PAT is successful

<u>IF TEAM A COMMITS A LOSS OF DOWN FOUL</u> during their successful PAT, cancel the score and no replay. If Team A's try is unsuccessful, any Team A penalty is automatically declined, and no replay.

<u>DURING A SUCCESSFUL PAT</u> where Team B fouls, Team A may choose to replay the down or keep the point(s) and have the penalty enforced on the kickoff. If the try is unsuccessful, enforce & replay the PAT.

<u>DOUBLE FOUL DURING A PAT</u>, replay the down.

<u>ON REPLAYS OF A PAT</u>, Team A's captain may designate where to re-snap between the hashes.

<u>THE TEAM WHO IS SCORED UPON DECIDES WHO KICKS OFF</u>. By rule, Team B may actually kick off. Why would they? Assume Team A just went ahead by 2 points. They will try to kick the ball deep. If Team B kicks off, they may on-side kick with a chance to get the ball around the 50.

Field goal

<u>A FIELD GOAL</u> is a place kick or drop kick through the uprights. A field goal may occur during any scrimmage down. A field goal may also occur after a fair catch or awarded fair catch (kickoff from a tee for 3).

<u>THE FIELD GOAL SHALL NOT TOUCH TEAM K</u> players beyond the expanded neutral zone (1st touching) or the ground before going through the uprights. If it touches Team R or an official in the end zone then caroms through the uprights, the field goal is good.

<u>THE FIELD GOAL SHALL GO THROUGH THE UPRIGHTS</u> or INSIDE the vertical plane above the uprights extended and above the crossbar.

THE TEAM SCORED UPON decides who kicks off.

FOULS DURING SUCCESSFUL FIELD GOAL BY TEAM R (except for non-player & unsportsmanlike) Team K may take the points off the board & play a scrimmage down again or keep the points and enforce the penalty on the kickoff.

USING AN ILLEGAL TEE on a field goal or PAT is an unfair act, **15 yards, basic spot foul.**

Force, safety & touchback

FORCE IS ENERGY that moves the ball from the field of play into the end zone. Force is blamed on the team that carries, snaps, passes, fumbles or kicks the ball. NEW force may occur on a grounded backward pass, fumble and kicks (but a non-scoring kick into Team R's end zone is ALWAYS a touchback). Touching or batting a pass, kick or fumble IN FLIGHT is NOT new force. (see definition "FORCE"). Forced touching is not touching.

SAFETY When Team A's runner doesn't advance the ball COMPLETELY out of his own end zone it is a safety, except in the case of momentum.

THE MOMENTUM EXCEPTION may occur during a change of possession (possessing a pass, fumble or kick) inside their own 5 yard line. If the momentum of the player possessing the ball carries him into his own end zone where the ball is declared dead, give it to him at the spot of change of possession inside the 5 yard line. It's not his fault he went in the end zone-the ball's force made him enter the end zone, so this isn't a safety if he's declared dead there. Momentum applies to all loose balls, even if the ball has hit the ground. A turnover that is possessed inside the 5 yard line and his original movement carries him into his end zone where the ball is declared dead, the ball is awarded on the yard line where the ball was possessed, inside the 5.

IT'S A SAFETY when a player loses possession in their end zone or forces a grounded loose ball from the field of play across their goal line and the ball becomes dead in his team's possession or goes out of bounds (except on legal forward passes).

IT'S A SAFETY when the offense commits a foul and the enforcement spot is in the end zone toward the end line. It is also a safety if Team A throws an illegal forward pass from their end zone (since this is treated like a running play).

IT IS A TOUCHBACK WHEN

***ANY kick goes into R's end zone, unless it is a field goal or PAT that may score

***A Team K player touches a field goal in R's end zone

***When Team K recovers their kick in their own end zone after Team R causes a NEW

FORCE on the grounded kick

***When a fumble or backward pass is sent across the goal line by an opponent after it has been grounded and this new bat/muff forces the ball across the goal line where a player who didn't force the ball recovers in their own end zone.

***When Team B intercepts the ball in their own end zone and they don't advance

FOR TOUCHBACKS, place the ball on the 20 yard line.

AFTER A SAFETY, place the ball on the 20 for the free kick.

CONDUCT OF PLAYERS & OTHERS

HELPING THE RUNNER-offensive player pushing the ball carrier-**5 yard spot foul.**

ILLEGAL USE OF HANDS/HOLDING-illegal blocking technique (see **"BLOCKING" definitions);** grasping/encircling a teammate to form interlocked blocking; using the arms or hands to hook/lock/clamp/hug or hold a non-runner; the runner grasping a teammate; adding to the momentum of charging defensive linemen on the line; contacting an eligible receiver that is no longer a potential blocker; Team B holding a non-runner-**10 yard (often) spot foul.**

ILLEGAL BLOCKING-A.K.A. kick catching interference, forward pass interference, personal fouls, etc**.-15 yard foul, enforcement spot varies.**

BLOCK BELOW THE WAIST **is illegal**, except in the free blocking zone; it's also OK to block the runner below the waist, or even a pretend runner-**15 yard, (often) spot foul.**

FAIR CATCH SIGNALER-can't block until the kick ends-**15 yard, PSK or all but 1 spot**

KICKER & HOLDER PROTECTION-on the kickoff, the kicker is protected until he advances 5 yards or the ball hits the ground or any player-**10 yard, previous spot foul.**

In scrimmage kicks, both are protected until they can recover-**running into=5 yards, roughing=15 yards + 1st down.**

CLIP & BLOCK IN THE BACK (see "**free blocking zone**" definition) some clips & blocks in the back are legal in the zone. The tackler may go through an opponent to tackle the runner or catch or recover a ball they may legally possess; it's also OK to clip/block runner below the waist.

CLIP is below the waist from behind-**15 yard, (often) spot foul.**

BLOCK IN THE BACK-(hands in the numbers above the waist)-**10 yard, (often) spot foul.**

CHOP BLOCK-a combination block by teammates both HIGH & LOW-**15 yards, (often) spot foul.**

TRIP-it's OK to trip the runner, but no one else-**15 yard, enforcement spot varies.**

TEAM K shall not block Team R on kickoffs until the ball crosses R's restraining line or Team R or unless R initiates the block-**10 yards, previous spot foul.**

ILLEGAL PERSONAL CONTACT (includes non-players)-15 yards each, spots vary

FIGHTING-a swing and a hit or miss with the leg or fist, locked hand/forearm/elbow or knee (fighting is not unsportsmanlike-it is a personal foul) **15 yds. + ejection.**

SWING A FOOT, SHIN OR KNEE into an opponent or extend the knee into a blocker.

CHARGE INTO OR THROW AN OPPONENT obviously out of the play.

GRASPING AND PULLING THE FACEMASK, MOUTH PIECE OR CHIN STRAP.

INTENTIONALLY CONTACTING AN OFFICIAL **15 + ejection.**

CONTACTING/THROWING AN OPPONENT TO GROUND after the ball is clearly dead.

ILLEGAL HELMET CONTACT against an opponent lying on the ground, against an opponent being held up by another, or illegal helmet contact against a defenseless player **15+ possible ejection**

SPEARING-(use of the helmet to punish an opponent)**15 + ejection.**

HORSE-TACKLE, (always treated as a live ball foul) grasping the inside collar or back of the shoulder pads or jersey of the runner and immediately pull them backward to the ground. **15 yards.**

ROUGHING THE PASSER-Team B must make an effort to avoid charging into the legal forward passer after it is CLEAR the ball has been released, including when he has released the legal forward pass and is fading back **15 yards + 1st down. Add it on to the end of the pass if beyond the LOS.**

RUNNING INTO THE KICKER-displacing=**5 yards, previous spot.**

ROUGHING KICKER/HOLDER-block, tackle or charge that is ROUGH-**15 yds. + 1st down, previous spot.**

IT IS NOT ROUGHING IF: the potential kicker is scrambling, kicks and is then contacted; when Team R touches the ball near the kick and his contact is unavoidable; there is slight contact (or kicker moves into the defender); or Team K blocks an R player into the kicker or holder.

ROUGHING THE SNAPPER-when in scrimmage kick formation, the snapper is protected from a DIRECT charge until he has time to recover-**15 yards + 1st down**

HITTING A HELMET-LESS PLAYER=**15 yard, personal foul**.

PLAYING WITHOUT THE HELMET=**illegal participation, basic spot foul**.

THESE ARE ALSO PERSONAL FOULS
TARGETING DEFENSELESS PLAYER (15 yards):

<u>PILING ON</u>

<u>HURDLE AN OPPONENT</u>
<u>BUTT BLOCK</u>

<u>FACE TACKLE</u>
<u>UNNECESSARY CONTACT</u>

<u>ON THE SHOULDERS OF A TEAMMATE</u>
<u>HIDING BALL UNDER THE SHIRT</u>
<u>USE OF HELMET TO RAM AN OPPONENT</u>
<u>SLAP A BLOCKER'S HEAD</u>
<u>THROWING A HELMET TO TRIP THE RUNNER</u>

NON-CONTACT UNSPORTSMANLIKE CONDUCT BY PLAYERS

These may be penalized once the officials take the field.

2 offenses=ejection. Enforce 15 yards from the succeeding spot.

<u>BAITING/TAUNTING</u> by acts/words/insignia that causes ill will, including taunting, acts that embarrass, ridicule, demean, and remarks about race, religion, gender or ethnicity.

<u>USING PROFANITY</u>, insulting/vulgar language & gestures.

<u>DRAWING ATTENTION TO SELF</u> in any delayed, prolonged or excessive act.

<u>TEAM B INTERFERING WITH TEAM A's SNAP COUNT</u> or shifts through acts or words.

<u>INTENTIONALLY KICKING THE BALL</u>, except as in a legal kick.

<u>LEAVING THE FIELD BETWEEN DOWNS</u> to gain an advantage.

<u>NOT FOLLOWING AN OFFICIAL'S INSTRUCTIONS.</u>

<u>TOBACCO USE.</u>

AFTER THE BALL IS DEAD THE RUNNER SHALL NOT: intentionally kick the ball; spike the ball; throw it up high; or fail to give it to an official or put it on the ground.

ILLEGAL PARTICIPATION-15 yards, various spots of enforcement

PLAYING WITHOUT A HELMET.

TEAM THAT INITIATES PLAY (A/K) CAN'T GO OUT OF BOUNDS & RETURN-unless blocked out-then he must return immediately. The official bean bags the spot where he accidentally or voluntarily went out, and flags the spot where he returns. If blocked out, no foul.

NO PLAYER MAY INTENTIONALLY GO OUT OF BOUNDS & RETURN.

PARTICIPATES OR TOUCHES THE BALL WHEN INTENTIONALLY OUT OF BOUNDS.

REPLACED PLAYER/SUBS CAN'T PARTICIPATE or influence the play.

12 PLAYERS ON FIELD IN FORMATION at the snap or free kick.

AN INJURED PLAYER DOESN'T SIT OUT one play, unless halftime or overtime occurs

PRETENDED SUBSTITUTION (water bucket play) at or immediately before the snap.

TO LIE ON THE GROUND AT THE SNAP/KICK to deceive opponents.

A DISQUALIFIED PLAYER RE-ENTERS THE GAME.

ILLEGAL BATTING/KICKING 15 yards & often a spot foul.

INTENTIONALLY KICKING THE BALL, except as in a legal kick.

BAT A LOOSE BALL, EXCEPT A BALL IN FLIGHT TO DEFLECT OR BLOCK IT.

A BALL IN POSSESSION MAY NOT BE BATTED FORWARD.

A BACKWARD PASS BY TEAM A CAN'T BE BATTED FORWARD by passing team.

EXCEPTIONS*: ANY IN FLIGHT BALL MAY BE LEGALLY BATTED; and TEAM K MAY BAT A SCRIMMAGE KICK, even in flight (to avoid a touchback), before it hits the ground and toward its own end-zone only; and TEAM K MAY BAT A GROUNDED KICKOFF to avoid a touchback.

UNSPORTSMANLIKE BY NON-PLAYERS 15 yards, succeeding spot foul.

NO COACH, TRAINER, SUB, OR ATTENDANT SHALL BE UNSPORTSMANLIKE.

PROFANITY, insulting remarks, vulgar language.

ATTEMPT TO INFLUENCE OFFICIAL'S DECISIONS or being disrespectful to an official, or objecting to an official's decision.

USING ILLEGAL COMMUNICATION EQUIPMENT No video, re-play, internet or TV usage.

HOLDING AN UNAUTHORIZED CONFERENCE, but players MAY come all the way to the sideline between plays (and during injury timeout) to talk to coaches off the field.

A TEAM NOT READY TO START EITHER HALF, including the 3 minute mandatory warm-up time.

PLAYERS WEARING OR USING ILLEGAL EQUIPMENT or not having all equipment.

A NON-PLAYER BEING ON THE FIELD, unless as a sub or replaced player.

TOBACCO USE.

BEING OUTSIDE THE TEAM BOX-replaced players & subs may exit the field on their side of the field away from the team box, but must head for it directly.

A SUBS ENTER DURING A FIGHT **eject each offender.**

DURING TIMEOUTS, including after the try, after a successful field goal, after a safety and before the following free kick, a team may hold an authorized conference. If it is held inside the numbers (9's) with one coach, 3 attendants (can't be uniformed athletes) may help their team. Attendants may also help their team when the Referee indicates. Be preventative, but if 4 come out or come out when they shouldn't, 1st offense is a 5 yard non-player foul, more is unsportsmanlike against the head coach.

4+ CAPTAINS AT THE COIN TOSS or having players on the field during the coin toss.

NON-PLAYERS SHALL STAY IN THE TEAM BOX, unless to sub or as a replaced player.

3 COACHES MAY BE IN THE COACHES BOX (6' area between the field & team box) but it must become empty when the snap is imminent. **1st offense=warning 2nd=sideline interference (5 yd. succeeding spot) 3rd+=unsportsmanlike and possible head coach ejection.**

EJECTED COACHES (2 offenses) must get beyond sight & sound of field & players.

MORE THAN 3 ATTENDANTS assisting the players, or assisting at the wrong time.

UNFAIR ACTS

No one shall hinder a player by an unfair act.

No team shall continually foul to ½ the distance to the goal line.

No player shall hide the ball under their jersey (**15 yard basic spot foul**).

No player shall use an illegal kicking tee (**no points, 15 yard basic spot foul**).

Neither team shall make a travesty of the game.

The Referee may award a score for an unfair act or any equitable penalty, or even forfeit the game.

> NOTE: Hiding the ball and using an illegal tee doesn't count as unsportsmanlike fouls toward a coach or player's disqualification.

PENALTY ENFORCEMENT

After fouls

<u>FOR LIVE BALL FOULS</u>, no whistle, officiate the play until the ball becomes dead. The Referee will then notify both Captains of the foul (by their signal to the press box) and may ask the offended Captain their option. The distance penalty may be declined. If the penalty is declined, the result of the play stands.

<u>DOUBLE FOUL</u>=no enforcement, replay the down.

<u>CAPTAIN'S CHOICE</u> can't be changed, and they must decide on options before any timeout. The only exception to this is the play following a fair catch or awarded fair catch, the Captain may choose to kick off from a tee for 3 points if a foul occurs on the next down.

<u>DEAD BALL FOULS</u> Officials will blow the whistle immediately to prevent the ball from becoming live. Enforce the foul from the succeeding spot, unless the distance penalty is declined (ex. on a PAT, Team K may decline an encroachment foul so they still kick from the 3 yard line and don't lose an angle the kicker likes).

<u>LIVE BALL + DEAD BALL FOUL</u> by the same team is not combined to make a multiple foul. A live ball + a dead ball foul by opponents is not combined to make a double foul. Enforce each foul separately, in order of occurrence.

<u>SAME TEAM COMMITS LIVE + DEAD BALL FOUL</u>-enforce all fouls.

<u>PENALTIES CAN'T BRING THE BALL</u> more than ½ the distance toward a goal line.

<u>LOSS OF DOWN FOULS FOR TEAM A (5 yards) each are fouls against the ball:</u>

Illegal forward pass Intentional grounding Illegal forward handing Illegal touch by ineligible

AUTOMATIC 1st DOWN

Roughing the passer/kicker/holder/snapper by Team B=**15 yard + automatic 1st down**.

If the passer is roughed and the pass is completed, **add 15 yards to end of the run.**

Double & multiple fouls

<u>REGULAR DOUBLE FOUL</u>-both teams have live ball fouls (not non-players or unsportsmanlikes) so penalties offset, with no change in team possession, replay the down.

PSK-don't combine PSK fouls and Team K fouls to make double fouls. PSK is a special enforcement. PSK enforcement applies to Team R fouls beyond the expanded neutral zone until the kick ends. These fouls are enforced where the kick is caught or recovered.

<u>CHANGE OF POSSESSION PLAYS</u>, Team B/K must decline penalty to keep the ball if the foul occurred before the change of possession.

Ex. Team A has an illegal shift. Team B recovers a fumble. **Ruling-Team B must decline the penalty to keep the ball.**

<u>ON CHANGE OF POSSESSION PLAYS</u>, with fouls by both teams, the "clean hands" rule applies. The team in final possession must have gotten possession legally, or without fouling-A.K.A. "clean hands." If Team B intercepts, but committed a foul before the change of possession, they have "dirty hands" A.K.A. they cheated then got the ball. Since they

cheated, they can't keep the ball. If Team A also committed a foul on this same play, it is a double foul, offset & re-play the down.

NOTE: PSK is an exception to the "clean hands" rule. If Team R fouls down field during the kick, they can keep possession, but their penalty is enforced from the PSK or "all but one" spot.

Ex. #1 Team A has illegal formation. Team B roughs the passer and intercepts. **Ruling=double foul-Team B has dirty hands when they intercepted, replay down**

Ex. #2 Team B has 12 on the field at the snap & recovers Team A's fumble. **Ruling=ball goes back to Team A, previous spot enforcement (illegal sub=5, illegal. participation.=15)**

Ex. #3 Team A has an illegal formation. Team B recovers a fumble then clips during the return. **Ruling=If Team B declines the illegal formation penalty, Team, B keeps the ball after their clip is enforced.**

Ex. #4 Team B intercepts a pass. During the return, Team A facemasks then Team B throws a punch (personal foul). **Ruling=Team B got the ball with clean hands, so they may keep the ball if they decline Team A's facemask, but their personal foul will be enforced and that player is ejected.**

Ex. #5 Same play as above, except take out the punch by Team B. **Ruling=Team B keeps the ball and the facemask is enforced.**

Ex. #6 Team K punts from the 50. Before the kick ends, R7 holds at the 30. Kick roll out at the 8. **Ruling=PSK enforcement, R's ball at the 4. Team R can maintain possession with dirty hands.**

<u>IF TEAM B intercepts</u> and during the return, both teams foul, Team B must decline A's foul, but Team B's foul is automatically enforced.

<u>MULTIPLE FOUL</u>=(2+ live ball fouls by the same team)-only one may be enforced, unless they are non-player or unsportsmanlike (enforce these at succeeding spot).

DEAD BALL FOULS Administer them all separately and in order of occurrence. DO NOT add live ball fouls to dead ball fouls to make multiple or double fouls.

Types of plays

LOOSE BALL MEANS:

Scrimmage kick, except for PSK enforcement
Free kick until there is possession
Legal forward pass plays (from snap until catch or incompletion)
Backward pass behind the line of scrimmage
Illegal kick or fumbles behind neutral zone until change of possession

RUNNING PLAY MEANS:

True running plays   Anything not mentioned above
The run after possessing a forward pass or kick or a fumble recovery or catch

THERE ARE OFTEN SEVERAL RUNNING PLAYS during a down. QB A1 receives snap, hands-off to RB A11 who advances, fumbles (beanbag), teammate recovers, advances=3 running plays.

THE END OF THE RUN is where the run ends. It may be the spot of the tackle, the spot of a fumble (beanbag) or spot of a catch or recovery on the momentum rule.

Basic spots

BASIC SPOT is sometimes the enforcement spot for Team A and Team B fouls.

THE BASIC SPOT IS THE PREVIOUS SPOT
(where ball was just snapped) ON:

Fouls simultaneous to the snap (illegal shift, formation, motion, sub)
Fouls on loose ball plays (legal forward passes, free kicks, fumble behind line of scrimmage)

Inadvertent whistle and the kick hasn't ended

THE BASIC SPOT IS WHERE THE RUN ENDED (tackle, fumble) ON RUNNING PLAYS

<u>ROUGHING THE PASSER</u> If the pass is completed, **add the penalty to the dead ball spot if it is beyond the LOS with no change of possession. If incomplete, previous spot enforcement.**

<u>PSK ENFORCEMENT</u> On fouls by **Team R beyond the neutral zone** (from the kick) until the kick ends are enforced from the spot where the kick was possessed or declared dead, or the "all but one" spot. PSK enforcement is an exception to the "clean hands" rule.

<u>SUCCEEDING SPOT ENFORCEMENT</u>=meaning where you were going to snap next, but a foul happened. It is the enforcement spot for ALL unsportsmanlike, non-player and dead ball fouls. When the play ends in a touchback and then there is a non-player, dead ball or unsportsmanlike foul, the enforcement spot is the 20.

<u>ON A CHANGE OF POSSESSION PLAY</u> where a run ends in a team's own end zone, force determines the enforcement. If A forced the ball into B's end zone, then the enforcement spot will be the 20. If B forces the ball into their own end zone and A fouls, the enforcement spot is the 20, even if a loose ball is declared dead in the field of play.

Ex. B intercepts in their own end zone, is face masked by A then fumbles to the 5. ***Ruling: The run ended in B's end zone and Team A forced it there with their pass, so enforce the facemask from the 20.***

Ex. #2 B recovers a fumble at the 7 and he carries it into his own end zone where he is face masked then fumbles to the 5 where the ball is declared dead.

Ruling: The run ended in B's end zone and, so enforce the face mask from the 20, B's ball on their 25 (for grasping) or 35 (for twisting & pulling) yard line.

Special enforcements

KICKOFF OUT OF BOUNDS Team R has 3 options: take the spot of the out of bounds kick; re-kick from 5 yards back or; take the ball 25 yards beyond the spot of the kick (usually the 35).

KICK CATCHING INTERFERENCE Team R may take an awarded fair catch at the spot or add a 15 yard penalty at the spot of the foul.

UNFAIR ACTS The Referee may award or disallow a score or do what he feels is fair.

GOOD PAT & TEAM B/R FOULS Team A/K may retry the point or enforce on the kickoff.

GOOD FIELD GOAL & FOUL BY TEAM B/R (other than unsportsmanlike or non-player) Team A/K may enforce from the basic spot or take points & enforce on the kickoff.

GOOD TOUCHDOWN & EITHER TEAM COMMITS NON-PLAYER OR UNSPORTSMANLIKE FOUL Opponents may apply it to the PAT or the kickoff.

UNSPORTSMANLIKE & NON-PLAYER fouls during scores have succeeding spot enforcement. If during a touchdown, either team's fouls may be enforced on the PAT or on the kickoff.

TEAM B FOULS ON A SACK IN TEAM A's END ZONE or ball declared dead there-mark off the penalty from the goal line.

TEAM A FOULS & SCORES = no score-mark off the penalty, unless it has succeeding spot enforcement from unsportsmanlike, non-player or dead ball fouls.

TEAM A THROWS AN ILLEGAL FORWARD PASS IN THEIR OWN END ZONE or commits foul in own end zone=**SAFETY**.

ROUGHING THE PASSER WHERE THE PASS WAS COMPLETE, **add 15 to the dead ball spot.**

<u>*DISQUALIFICATION*</u>-remove the player from the rest of the game.

PENALTY CHART

<u>5 YARD PENALTIES (LOD=loss of down)</u>

Not wearing equipment correctly	Incidental face mask	Delay of game
Attendant illegally on field	Sideline interference	Illegal formation
Incorrect equipment at snap	Helping the runner	Encroachment
Non-player not in team box	Numbering requirement	False start
Illegal forward handing (LOD)	Illegal touching (LOD)	Intentional grounding (LOD)
Illegal forward pass (LOD)	Illegal substitution	Illegal snap
Kickoff infraction (not b/t hash)	Kickoff out of bounds	Less than 7 on A's line
Invalid/illegal fair catch signal	Planned loose ball	Illegal motion/shift
Running into kicker/holder	Ineligible downfield	

<u>10 YARD PENALTIES</u>

Interlocked blocking	Illegal blocking	Illegal K block on kickoff
Runner grasping teammate	Illegal block in the back	Illegal use of hands & Holding

<u>15 YARD PENALTIES (LOD=loss of down) A1D=automatic 1ˢᵗ down)</u>

Charging opponent out of play	Unsportsmanlike conduct	Butt blocking
Illegal kicking/batting	Illegal participation	Chop block
Roughing passer (A1D)	Roughing kicker (A1D)	Roughing snapper (A1D)
Grasping/pulling facemask	Kick catching interference	Roughing holder (A1D)
Non-player illegally on field	Illegal personal contact	Head slap

Illegal block after FC signal	Face tackling	Tripping
3rd (+) Sideline interference	A Pass Interference	Clipping
B Pass Interference	Blocking below the waist	
Blocking protected kicker/holder	Horse Collar Tackle	

15 YARDS + EJECTION

Contact official intentionally	Fighting	Spearing
Kneeing/striking/kneeing	Flagrant fouls	2nd Unsportsmanlike
Unnecessary (flagrant) roughness	Leaving box to fight	

PENALTY ENFORCEMENT

(unless there is a special enforcement like PSK, roughing passer, change of possession, TD, etc . . .)

ALL BUT ONE PRINCIPLE

Many fouls are enforced from the basic spot, but there is an **ALL BUT ONE PRINCIPAL**. It states, unless there is a special enforcement stated above, enforce Team A penalties from the basic spot unless there is a Team A foul behind that basic spot.

<u>*A FOUL BY TEAM A BEHIND THE BASIC SPOT* **IS ENFORCED FROM THE SPOT OF THE FOUL OR THE END OF THE RUN, *WHICHEVER IS WORSE!***</u>

<u>*Penalize the offense from the spot that hurts them the most!*</u>

Ex. #1 Team A snaps at their 30 and holds at their own 25 on a legal forward pass. **Ruling=the basic spot (pass is loose ball play) is the previous spot, but the spot of the foul is behind the basic spot, so enforce 10 yards from the spot of the foul, ball at the 15.**

Ex. #2 Team A snaps at the 50. At A's 45, A1 fumbles. At the 40, Team A holds. The ball is recovered by Team A at the 30. **Ruling=back them up 10 yards from the 30 unless Team B declines the penalty. Loose ball foul, but the "all but one" principle is in effect.**

Ex. #3 The ball is snapped from Team K's 35. K4, the punter, fumbles the snap. The "up back" holds at the 30 and the kick is made. Team R fair catches at their own 40. **Ruling=if Team R accepts the penalty-10 yards from the 30. The basic spot is the previous spot, but K's hold was behind the basic spot.**

Ex. #4 Team A snaps from Team B's 20. They attempt a sweep but it is a bad pitch at the 30. A3 blocks below the waist at the 35 and recovers the ball at the 40. **Ruling=the end of the run is now the 40-back them up 10 yards from the end of the run.**

Ex. #5 R9 receives a scrimmage kick at their 20. Before the kick ended, R59 held the gunner at the 30. R9 tries unsuccessfully to avoid the tackler and is downed at their 12. **Ruling=the PSK spot is the 20, but his run ended behind the PSK spot. Enforce the hold half the distance from the 12 to the 6 yard line.**

Made in the USA
San Bernardino, CA
05 September 2014